D1360277

What others are saying about *Restoring Hope Across America*

Restoring Hope Across America is an inspiring book that all Americans should read. We owe it to future generations to "right the sinking ship...through civic leadership, personal courage, and moral persuasion." Americans must ask themselves, "For what do we stand and what do we want to do about it?" This book clearly states the concerns of many Americans as well as why civic leadership is desperately needed, and that we must work to reclaim and preserve the American dream for future generations.

Jerry C. Davis, President, College of the Ozarks

America is blessed with an exceptional military and hurt by far too many deceitful politicians. Having served in the US military for over two decades and six years in politics, Major Duff has seen the best and worst of both worlds. He honorably served in defense of our nation and now has gone on the offense to take on politicians who do not have our best interests at heart. Restoring Hope Across America is a must read for concerned citizens who want to make a positive, genuine impact in our shattered political arena.

Melony Butler
Founder, Eagle's Healing Nest

Two generations have now been raised with minimal appreciation for our nation's spiritual heritage. The US needs a revival in the hearts and minds of American's if we are to reclaim America in accordance with our national motto "as one nation, under God." Restoring Hope Across America is a fantastic read for those wanting America back as home of the brave and land of the free!

Reverend Dr. Kenneth L. Beale, Jr.
Chaplain (Colonel-Ret) U.S. Army

Major Duff hits the nail on the head in this book. It seems partisan politics has replaced doing what is good and proper for the people. Unfortunately, it is both political parties working to gain advantage in campaigns and elections at the expense of solving problems, and hard-working Americans lose out. Alan Duff effectively articulates how this is harming our nation and offers freedom-loving citizens practical steps to fix it.

Denny Schulstad
Retired Air Force Brigadier General & Former Minneapolis
City Councilmember

Restoring

Hope

Across

America

Alan Duff

CONTENTS

I. Introduction   1

II. Privileges   8

    1.   The Greatest Experiment in Human History   10

    2.   One Nation, Under God   16

    3.   Freedom Is Our Friend   23

    4.   Prosperity in Abundance   29

    5.   The Right to Speak Your Mind   34

    6.   Trusting Citizens with Our Second Amendment   41

    7.   Civic Support of Our Core Values   45

III. Challenges   52

    8.   American Values Under Attack   55

    9.   Who Can We Trust?   62

    10.   Misunderstanding the Priorities of Politicians   69

    11.   The Unhealthy Expansion of Public Gluttony   75

    12.   Citizens Held Hostage to Political Power   81

    13.   Undermining National Unity via Political Correctness   87

    14.   Replacing Public Order with Chaos   93

    15.   A Future of Doom and Gloom   100

IV. Opportunities   105

    16.   It All Starts with Civic Leadership   111

    17.   Bringing Morals Back into Our Culture   119

    18.   Pushing Back on Political Gluttony   128

    19.   Regaining Our Lost Government   135

    20.   Bringing Hope to the Next Generation   141

V. Conclusion   147

NOTES   155

About the Author   159

I.

Introduction

The design of America was arguably one of the greatest experiments ever created by humankind. The principle of limited government with appropriate checks and balances established a nation with a remarkable, incredible more than 240-year history. The basic foundation of prioritizing individual freedom over a large powerful government has fostered human ingenuity in so many ways that define the great American experiment as an overwhelming success to date.

That great American design, as articulated through the Constitution, Declaration of Independence, and Bill of Rights, ensured the creation of a very special nation. So who would want to overhaul the greatest experiment in human history? Certainly other nations that want to undermine our power, but they have existed since our founding. However, I believe America has a challenging enemy that lies within, specifically:

Self-serving politicians and their accomplices who care more about personal power and short-term gain than genuine service to those they are elected to serve are the greatest threat to America's future (accomplice is described as "a person who works with or helps someone who is doing something wrong or illegal" according to Merriam Webster Collegiate Dictionary, 11ᵗʰ Edition).

The foundational values that hold Americans together are under attack. Americans are losing hope that their government can solve even the simplest problems. A nation built on independence and self-reliance is being overhauled into one of dependence that "helps" its citizens through an ever-growing list of programs and initiatives that offer a weak return on investment for the hardworking taxpayers of this great nation.

We must regain what was most special about our government before it's too late. With the average person paying taxes to more than a dozen different governmental jurisdictions, this problem is very wide and very deep at many levels, including in our federal, state, and local governments. In fact, I believe our nation focuses too much energy on what any president does or doesn't do, so we miss out on many of the governmental challenges facing us. Please note, this book will be nonpartisan as I focus on preserving the United States of America, not dividing the nation by party or personality. The blame-the-other-party approach has not been effective in solving many of the great challenges before us.

Americans' frustration over political lies and constant blame games is at a boiling point. Never-ending efforts to divide us by political party or other classifications are destroying our core identity. Many of us are aware that civic engagement is critical, but knowing what steps we can take to regain what has been lost in our once-great government is overwhelming to many of us, particularly frustrated citizens who feel this is no longer "their government." Wouldn't it be wonderful if our politicians valued service toward others rather than expanding their personal or political power?

As I discussed in my first book, *Fixing America's Shattered Politics*, the military is one credible organization to emulate for its honorable public service principles, which are sorely needed in many political circles. Unfortunately, we find ourselves in a time of power struggles, when far too many within political circles do not agree that the primary role of "public service" should embody accountability and honorable service to others over self. Shouldn't our politicians be accountable for their actions, just as people in other professions must?

The basic American priorities of God, family, and country are being replaced by many with the loudest voices who emphasize government, celebrities, and rights as the new priorities that embody our ever-evolving national identity. Rights are important to protect, as long as they are balanced with the reality of consequences. Celebrities may be gifted in entertaining us, but are they truly the voices that should most loudly represent mainstream America? And replacing God with government as the leading force of our nation would adversely change the character and cultural identity of America.

Americans are looking for hope in turning around the mess in which they find themselves. Many are eagerly looking for ways to restore the foundational values that blessed our nation for so long but now seem lost in our new cultural identity. It is time to empower the individual, including their faith and family, over politicians. Demanding more entitlements from the government not only isn't working, it's destroying our once-strong, resilient nation. Religion and family are not perfect, but they have a much stronger track record of helping solve challenges than our politicians, who are often more interested in appeasing than delivering strong results that are provided efficiently and within budget. Families, businesses, and houses of worship are expected to operate within budgets and limits, and we should demand that government put forth at least a good faith effort to do the same.

Just what does it take to be a "great American"? And why is it important that we identify the qualities embodied in that description? Certainly, as with any successful organization, there are different parts of America that come together to make it more effective. As Americans continue to look at their identity, there will be continued debate about this question. One leadership skill taught in the military to help us understand our responsibilities to ourselves, our team, and our nation was the Crawl, Walk, Run principle:

Crawl—Carefully building our core values is foundational to building strong character. It gives us the courage to do what is right, regardless of the circumstances or consequences. As part of Crawl, we should be aware of our personal core values as well as our country's values.

Walk—Knowledge and skills are needed to be a competent leader. Military officers are taught that mastery of knowledge and skills is essential to success in creating positive change.

Run—Leaders act. They bring together everything they are, everything they believe, and everything they know how to do to provide purpose, direction, and motivation. This involves the following three leader actions: influencing, operating, and improving.

Utilizing the Crawl, Walk, Run principle, Americans can identify their personal attributes and use them to make positive contributions to the communities in which they live. When soldiers truly understand the depths of their own character, that knowledge provides them with the courage and motivation to overcome difficult challenges. This is instrumental in helping our nation's military overcome intense adversity. This principle can also be an effective change agent in helping Americans realize their personal convictions in a manner that motivates them to take positive steps to improve their communities as they understand the changes necessary and the decisive actions they must take before it is too late. The Crawl attribute, for example, helped me have the courage to stand up against immoral, illegal, and unethical political endeavors numerous times during my time as a county commissioner.

The second leadership step is to be knowledgeable about a particular subject matter. In civics, being knowledgeable means having at least a basic understanding of the many political organizations that have the legal authority to govern you and your family. Because the average American has anywhere from ten to twenty or more governmental bodies with a taxing authority over them, understanding every political body can be overwhelming. An effective civic leader understands the primary role of these political bodies, which helps them be a strong voice in ensuring that the genuine job of public stewardship is undertaken to prevent the political shenanigans that benefit self-serving politicians at a great cost to we the people. It is helpful to know the roles of these different governmental agencies, which are technically there to serve us.

The first two steps of "to be" and "to know" are essential in empowering individuals to become effective leaders; however, they can't be effective without doing something about it. The Run step allows leaders to influence, operate, and improve situations around them. In a country where most Americans complain about some level of political incompetence, corruption, or cronyism, a strong group of citizens who have personal integrity and courage, knowledge about the principles that comprise our great nation, and a "can-do" attitude to take the actions necessary to change our political climate for the better are necessary, acting one community at a time across our nation.

What are the political principles and practices essential to the American culture? The answers to this question may vary significantly, but most of us agree that there is a strong disconnect between political promises and actual results, particularly results that serve the overall public good. That same disconnect exists between the politician and the average citizen. Like many others, I continue to be amazed to read about political votes on issues that have little to do with real-life public concerns and it's no wonder we become frustrated that our basic interests of security, transparency, and limited government have disappeared because so many politicians have a much different agenda.

To overcome this political dysfunction, we will need more citizens to understand and apply the Crawl, Walk, Run principles to their own lives:

- Crawl—Be an informed American by knowing your rights and responsibilities;

- Walk—Know what is happening to take away these rights and privileges; and

- Run—Do something about it within your personal sphere of influence.

Rather than discussing political party or personality nuances, this book will focus on how we can regain real American values that bring respect and honor back into the public sector at many levels. The three main sections of this book, which will help you on your journey to being all you can be as a civic-minded American, are:

- Privileges—Of being American and the gifts we have inherited;

- Challenges—Why these gifts are dangerously close to being taken away from the next generation; and

- Opportunities—For each individual to make a positive impact on our country's future.

Most books on politics have an agenda or bias. Here is mine:

- I love America's foundation of freedom and liberty, but I am very concerned for the future of our great nation;

- I have great respect and admiration for our military and the sacrifices they undertake to keep our nation safe;

- We need political leaders who, regardless of political party or ideology, will work together for the good of the people as they are sworn to do in their oaths of office;

- We need more selfless elected officials who will fight for their constituents rather than focusing on their own agendas; and

- My priority in addressing shattered politics is not Red (Republican) nor Blue (Democrat), my priority is advocating for a united Red, White, and Blue America!

It is time to bring this nation back to the hardworking citizens who deserve a country they can proudly call the home of the free because of the brave.

II.

Privileges

Patriotism is supporting your country all the time, and your government when it deserves it.

—Mark Twain, American Writer, 19th century

American citizenship has very special privileges that many of us often take for granted. Unfortunately, sometimes it takes a catastrophe or a serious life moment to alert us to the blessings all around us. Let's not wait for a catastrophe; let's pause now, take a look around, and see just how blessed we are to live in this incredible nation. We have so much to be thankful for as we live the American dream each and every day!

As we identify what each of us can do to "be all we can be" in shaping this citizen-led nation, I believe our passions and energies best come to life when we fully grasp the special privileges we have as American citizens. Like all nations throughout the world, America has its problems. However, as we saw in the days and weeks following the September 11, 2001, attack, our nation is particularly good at coming together during difficult times. Not only coming together, but also resolving to take on adversity in many strong and powerful ways. That value of the American spirit has the power to unite us despite the differences we may have. Yes, even political, personality, religious, and family differences.

During my twenty-three years of service in the US military, I was taught, and often reminded, what an honor it is to defend such a special ideal as the United States of America. This nation I defended was and still is defined as special because it is governed by unique principles: maintaining a limited government that minimizes intrusion into the lives of its citizens; the protection of civil and religious rights; and, of course, freedom, liberty, and justice for all. Simply put, the American way is truly special!

My military training was so impactful and uplifting because it encouraged service members to be willing to make sacrifices, both great and small, for the honor of defending our nation against all enemies, foreign and domestic. Many are willing to sacrifice much, including the ultimate sacrifice. They do it for their God and their family. In the military, we learn that defending the American way is an honor and a privilege, and we willingly take those responsibilities very seriously.

Thus, when we assess what is worth the fight, I would like to encourage you to consider the following. How do we preserve the American dream for future generations? This is of the utmost importance, especially in a time when civic leadership is desperately needed in communities across the country. It is needed to allow us to work diligently to reclaim and preserve the American dream for future generations.

What do you like about being an American? As we ponder the vast number of privileges of living the American way, let's remember we have inherited a very special gift. It is an honor and a privilege to identify our individual opportunities, which we're responsible for preserving, restoring, and passing along as invaluable assets. In the next several chapters, I will discuss some of the incredible privileges we have as American citizens to remind us of our past and help set the tone for where we can be most effective in our own unique, personal ways in shaping the future.

★★★▬▬ QUESTIONS TO PONDER

- What do you think it means to be a great American?

- How will the collective voices of mainstream America affect our nation's future?

- What do you think the American dream will look like over the next several decades?

1. The Greatest Experiment in Human History

We hold these truths to be self-evident, that all men are created equal, that they are endowed by their Creator with certain unalienable rights; that among these are life, liberty, and the pursuit of happiness.

—excerpt from the Declaration of Independence

It can be difficult to appreciate things we cannot see. Yet some of the greatest things in life are invisible attributes we feel in our hearts, like faith, love, and a sense of belonging within a community. Finding and embracing intangible qualities that align with our personal interests is important for all of us because it gives us a deeper sense of meaning and purpose in life. The design of America was guided by freedom and liberty, but the power of these principles can be hard to comprehend unless we are able to make a personal connection to these values and recognize how they apply to our own lives. We are at a turbulent time in America, when the working definition of American citizenship is being debated in many public and private forums. At challenging times like this, it is important to look closely at the following question:

What does it mean to be an American, and what privileges does this extend to each of us?

If we are going to accept something we cannot see, we must be able to define it and understand why this attribute is valuable for our own lives, as well as the lives of our loved ones. This is especially important if we are going to consider defending these intangible values within our circle of family, friends, and neighbors. Just as in faith or contractual relationships such as marriage, it is critical that we understand the oath we are taking as American citizens to support these commitments. The oath of American citizenship is defined by the US Citizenship and Immigration Services as a pledge of allegiance to our Constitution and our way of life, and prospective citizens are required to pass a test on American civics as well.[1] An oath of allegiance to any cause is a serious proposition, and American citizenship is no different.

So what makes this place called the United States of America so special? Each of us will undoubtedly answer this question differently based on our own unique life experiences. For me, there are many aspects that make

America the greatest experiment ever designed in human history. These aspects were reinforced to me often during my twenty-three years of US military service, reminding me that we were defending something truly special. We were reminded frequently that America is distinct from all other countries in its founding and in the values, rights, and privileges it confers upon its citizens. The following are some of the key privileges of American citizenship. You may want to reflect on how they relate to your own personal values.

- A legal framework that respects and protects the individual dignity of all citizens;

- Openness to religious differences;

- Equal opportunity for all to pursue the American dream;

- Guaranteed right of free expression (First Amendment);

- Guaranteed right to bear arms and protect oneself (Second Amendment);

- Prosperity that can be built through hard work, risk-taking, and capitalism;

- Freedom for each individual to choose the path they wish to take in life;

- Liberty and justice that is fair for the individual while protecting the public welfare;

- Incredible geographic setting with an abundance of natural resources; and

- Defense of our nation by a strong, first-class military.

Let's take a brief look at each of these American values.

Respect and protection for all citizens: The founding of America came with a new design in governance, a legal framework that emphasizes and protects the right to be self-governed. That means that each of us has a right, a privilege, and even a responsibility to speak up on the future of our nation, starting in our own communities. This was rare in world history because it was specifically created with protections provided in writing in our Constitution as the law of the land. The Constitution gives each of us the privilege of protecting ourselves from an unaccountable government. It established checks and balances to minimize the abuse of public power, to provide a country where the human spirit can reach its highest potential.

Worship as we choose: Some of our founding fathers escaped significant religious persecution, which made them intent on establishing a new nation guided by protective measures for religious expression. That means citizens of the United States can follow their religious beliefs without political pressure or persecution to believe one way or another. Throughout world history, a nation that embraces the privilege of free worship is truly unique. American citizens are not told what, who, or how to believe in their faith, but are given free will to pursue and choose their faith as they desire.

Fairness over favoritism: The development of virtually all nations was predicated on a strong bias toward the ruling class. In contrast, the design of America established it as a place with equal opportunity for all to pursue their dreams to the best of their abilities. Though not perfect, America offers its citizens a fairer opportunity to succeed than most nations, where cronyism and relationships with rulers are often far more important factors than productivity and the ability to produce market-driven results.

First Amendment protection: American citizens are able to speak their mind, peaceably assemble, and petition their government for a redress of grievances. We have a voice in our governance.

Second Amendment protection: American citizens are strongly protected in their right to keep and bear arms to protect themselves and their families.

Prosperity: The survival of a nation involves meeting the basic needs of food and shelter, and America has done better than most as a place where rags-to-riches stories are quite common. What separates us from most other nations is the high level of prosperity created by capitalism, personal motivation, and a cultural mind-set that supports entrepreneurial risk-taking and creativity in producing products and services that compete locally, as well as in the world economy. Many of us are truly spoiled by prosperity and have the opportunity to give generously to those in need as we choose.

Freedom to choose our own paths: In the traditional establishment of governments around the world, rights are identified, prioritized, and then given by the government to the people. In America, the government was designed in an opposite fashion, as citizens identified very limited rights that were given by the people to the government. This juxtaposition of power in the people is truly the hallmark of the American idea. The United States would be a land of freedom and opportunity, with minimal government intrusion and a limited central government that would protect the people by maintaining a safe environment in which they could pursue happiness as they saw fit. A governance based on freedom of choice is predicated on the fact that it allows us to pursue success, as well as the opportunity to fail and learn from our mistakes.

Liberty and justice for all: Our founding fathers designed a form of government that was accountable to the people, leaving them fundamentally in charge of their own destinies, which they wisely believed would best protect human liberty. Justice is delivered fairly to those breaking these rules, with the presumption of innocence until proven guilty by a jury of one's peers. The American way of establishing laws designed to be minimally intrusive and a fair and impartial judgment of those breaking the law is quite special.

Courageous sacrifice over self: America's history of selfless sacrifice by many brave men and women in preserving our foundational principles has kept these many unique values in place throughout our nation's history. When things are going well, it is easy for most organizations to plug along and keep going; however, the natural rule of law is that there are ups and downs in the cycle of life. America has faced some incredible challenges—a civil war in the nineteenth century, two world wars in the twentieth century, and the attack on our nation in the twenty-first century. In response to these challenges, as well as others, Americans came together, put aside their petty differences, and did what was best for the country. America has evolved into the incredible land of the free and the home of the brave.

Our founding fathers' design for America is arguably the greatest experiment ever in human history, and the privileges associated with this foundation are still relevant today. While this notion is being challenged, including by some in leadership positions, when one looks at our country's history objectively, it is hard to dispute how remarkable its journey has been and the impact it has had on human history.

> *The message for the American youth is that this is a great country and we need to make sure that we pass on a heritage, a lineage and a legacy of American exceptionalism to each and every one of you so that you can enjoy all the great liberties and freedoms that all the previous generations have had.*
> —Allen West, former US Representative and Retired US Army Lieutenant Colonel

★★★ ══ QUESTIONS TO PONDER

- What do you think is the greatest privilege of American citizenship?

- Why do you think America can or cannot be defined as the greatest experiment in human history?

- Which American privilege is in most danger of being taken away?

2. One Nation, Under God

I pledge allegiance to the flag, of the United States of America. And to the Republic, for which it stands, one nation, under God, indivisible, with liberty and justice for all.
—The Pledge of Allegiance

All nations are designed by public policy and laws, which are established to promote some form of civil order and function. Typically, these laws are created by the rulers of a nation based on some semblance of laws from previously established nations. America was founded and designed much differently. As a civic-led government, America established its laws in a manner that protects citizens from a government that might try to limit their religious, personal, and other freedoms, while at the same time determining standards of moral conduct that would foster public good. Our nation's founders took the blessings of religious affiliation away from the government and put them into the hands and hearts of each citizen.

As America is the longest-running constitutional republic in the world, it is important to look at what motivated our nation's founders to design a country with such durable values. To set the context, we need to remember that many of America's founding fathers left their motherland primarily because of religious persecution, and one of their top goals in establishing a new nation was to protect religious liberty for all. Specifically, early American design was based on allowing its citizens the free opportunity to express themselves religiously however they chose. Over time, American citizens have become accustomed to living without religious restraints, forgetting how unique this principle is. Americans are blessed with the opportunity to choose their understanding of and commitment to their faith as they wish, which speaks loudly to our core individualistic spirit. Americans can choose how much religion factors into our lives.

At the core of the legal protection for America's citizens is the principle found in the Establishment Clause in the First Amendment, stating that the United States will not create a national religion. This legal standard protects us from having to live under a government mandate that specifies a national religious belief. This means that any religion that has laws backing its doctrine would not be acceptable as the national religion. In other words, the rights of individuals to worship God as they choose are endless, as long as this religious expression does not harm other individuals or undermine the Constitution.

Like many people, my views on faith have changed over the years, and I am grateful to live in a nation that allows me the liberty to embrace these changes in a personal and meaningful manner. As in all decisions we make, we need to remember there are consequences to our actions. When citizens choose to reject common societal standards of conduct, it almost always results in lower public productivity. With this in mind, America's founders designed a structure based on the delicate balance of establishing religious liberty for its citizens while setting up social expectations that would be most productive for a new, growing nation.

The founders of our nation clearly articulated that positive moral habits were important in creating a greater potential for political and economic prosperity. Such a nation is most sustainable and emphasizes productivity while minimizing public costs. This basic principle helped build a foundation of wealth, security, and freedom for a new nation to grow and sustain itself against intrusions by other nations. The moral standard desired for a new nation was communicated early on by three of its leaders:

> *Of all the dispositions and habits which lead to political prosperity, religion and morality are indispensable supports. Reason and experience both forbid us to expect that natural morality can prevail in exclusion of religious principles.*
> —President George Washington, during his farewell address
> to Congress at the end of his second term

> *Our constitution was made only for a moral and religious people. It is wholly inadequate to the government of any other.*
> —John Adams, the first vice president and second president of
> the United States

> *The Bible and liberty are close companions. You cannot successfully have one without the other. Religion and good morals are the only solid foundation of public liberty and happiness.*
> —Samuel Adams, American statesman and
> political philosopher

Establishing laws based on a moral code is very difficult for a nation of diverse people who do not want to be told what to do by virtually anyone, but it is necessary for public order and function. I remember thinking, as a college student, how rules got in the way of my living life the way I wanted. Yet I quickly learned how an organized code of conduct provided structure and direction when I entered military service, where rules and discipline were so important. Getting used to following military rules was very difficult for this stubborn person, but I learned in the end that it was best for me, even as an individual. The rules and discipline that guide US service members are what make us the strongest military in the world. Individuals quickly learn to give up some of their personal identity for the betterment of the common good. But how does this relate to "one Nation, under God," you may ask? Allowing freedom of religious expression for a citizenry is a very valuable right, but pushing the boundaries of right and wrong in the name of religious freedom can have costly consequences, as we know from the Branch Davidians, the Jonestown massacre, and other cult tragedies.

Anyone who investigates the most-cited sources in our nation's founding documents will find that the Scriptures were one of the most common references for establishing the ideal morals. This does not mean you have to be Christian to live in this country, but it does mean the Bible, both Old and New Testaments, was an important resource for the founders of the United States. The foundation of America was based on many moral characteristics that, taken in their original context, set a high standard of conduct. For example, that liberty and justice are guaranteed for all is a lofty standard to strive for, and America has come closer to reaching it than most nations.

As I reviewed the spiritual heritage of America and assessed how biblical principles were incorporated into key legal structures of our nation to write this book, I believe the foundation of this nation was built during our first two hundred years based in large part on these fundamental Judeo-Christian values:

- Honest hard work benefits both the individual and the communities affected by it.

- Individuals are more likely to follow a moral code if they come to an understanding of their faith of their own free will rather than by government mandates.

- A nation has an obligation to protect obedient citizens from illegal behaviors that undermine the public good.

- America should foster charity by supporting the opportunity for citizens to give to the needy as they freely choose on their own, not as dictated by the government via taxation (emphasis on individual generosity instead of public confiscation of tax dollars to support causes supported by political influencers).

- Humility is critical for future governance as Americans realize that the rules of God are more applicable, time-tested, and valuable than the rules of man.

Following our involvement in two world wars, our nation looked reflectively at what was important, and another two steps in our declaration as a nation were forthcoming. In 1945, the official name of "The Pledge of Allegiance" was adopted, and on Flag Day 1954, the words *under God* were added after the words *one nation*. America's religious culture was furthered in 1956, when Congress established "In God We Trust" as the official motto of the United States. These two declarations solidified the foundation set by our founding fathers, who established this nation based on the belief that we have certain inalienable rights that are endowed by our Creator. Recognizing that our inalienable rights are given to us by God, and not government, is a unique distinction between the United States and many other nations. We may disagree over the exact identity of our Creator, but recognizing that our rights derive from a higher power is critical to understanding the fundamental American value that God is more powerful than government. Having the individual freedom to worship—or not to worship—God however one chooses is a blessing for all Americans.

Americans working together as one nation under God gives us the blessings of individual independence to worship as we choose, combined with a strong moral compass. With this foundation, our nation had a beautiful win-win future of both liberty and prosperity. We will see how morals affect society differently, but the following are a few of the things I believe were critical in setting our nation off on the right foot and preserving it for many years:

- The freedom to worship God as one individually chooses is a key right and privilege of being an American.

- Honorably serving others provides better public value than selfish actions.

- Our society functions better when moral standards are in place to guide beneficial public behaviors and citizens are given a second chance, if necessary.

- Life is precious and worthy of protection.

- America permits citizens the privilege of freely pursuing happiness in their own way(s), not the guarantee that they will be happy.

- What is identified as a priority for charitable giving is a highly individualistic decision, and the Constitution is designed to protect us from the abuse of public officials confiscating funds for questionable charitable activities.

- There are always consequences to our actions, or our inactions, including both our individual and public moral behaviors.

Great values are foundational to any successful organization, and I would contend that America's traditional values are profound, are liberating to the human spirit, and have withstood the test of time. Our nation's religious values are based on proven principles that liberate the human spirit to pursue our dreams and result in a solid foundation for this great nation. The better we comprehend the amazing blessings of these principles, the stronger our convictions will be in doing our individual and collective parts to preserve these incredible values moving forward.

> *There is no country in the whole world in which the Christian religion retains a greater influence over the souls of men than in America—and there can be no greater proof of its utility, and of its conformity to human nature, than its influence is most powerfully felt over the most enlightened and free nation of the earth.*
>
> —Alexis de Tocqueville, *Democracy in America*

★★★══ QUESTIONS TO PONDER

- Why is it important today to know that our founders believed our inalienable rights were derived from God and not government?

- What does separation of church and state mean to you?

- How do the immoral actions of individuals negatively affect communities?

- What standards of moral conduct have you found important in guiding your personal, family, educational, and business life?

3. Freedom Is Our Friend

A friend is someone who gives you total freedom to be yourself.
—Jim Morrison, American singer and songwriter

Have you ever thought about what freedom truly means and why it is valuable in your everyday life? For many, freedom is important simply because they do not want to be controlled by others against their wishes. As we are a nation of highly independent citizens, freedom is the framework that allows us to maintain our independence.

This is a definition of freedom I use frequently:

> *Freedom is having the opportunity to speak, act, and pursue happiness without unnecessary external restrictions. Freedom is critical to the American way because it leads individuals to greater levels of creativity and original thought, increased productivity, and overall higher quality of life. Freedom is our friend.*

Freedom is truly our friend in America, and the value of this gift cannot be overstated. It is the foundation that gives us the ability to live as we choose. We must remain diligent in protecting freedom with our passionate voices because this gift can easily be taken away from us, as recent history from around the world shows, such as the 2017 Catalonia attempt to vote for an independence referendum in Spain that was thwarted by Madrid police, resulting in nearly nine hundred injuries.[2] As President Ronald Reagan once stated, "Freedom is never more than one generation away from extinction."

Freedom is fundamentally a byproduct of identifying who has power and control, and in America, the two groups competing for power are the citizens and those who govern them, our politicians. These two groups have gone back and forth in establishing America's varying levels of freedom, but for the most part, our history is flavored with tremendous amounts of freedom thanks to effective civic leadership. The most valued types of freedoms embraced by American citizens are typically defined in this order of importance: freedom of speech, due process rights, the right to keep and bear arms, free exercise of religion, and voting rights. The following are additional examples of the freedoms we have come to expect at high levels:

- Ability to participate freely in the political process;

- Ability to worship or not worship as we wish;

- Ability to assemble and associate freely for causes we believe in;

- Ability to learn in schools and public libraries;

- Ability to have access to an established, equitable system of rule of law and to be assumed innocent in trials until proven otherwise;

- Ability to own private property;

- Ability to freely bring talents to the marketplace as an employee or employer;

- Ability to serve, or not serve, in the military; and

- Ability to access assistance to help overcome disabilities.

Have you ever thought how your life would be affected if some of these freedoms were taken away? Another way of looking at the incredible value of freedom is to assess the painful costs against our basic human rights when freedom really is taken away. These costs can have devastating impacts on our individual morale, as well as the overall well-being of our society. Some examples of these costs can be determined when we ask the following questions:

- How do limits on our freedom of speech restrict the opportunity we have to learn from one another or to be able to speak out against dangerous actions?

- How would you feel about our government if our political leaders used force to limit voting privileges?

- How would you feel if your government told you public input was not allowed by a public body to whom you pay taxes?

A government with minimal powers that provides individuals the free opportunity to make as many of their own choices as possible is a great idea. As we've seen, that was what our founding fathers envisioned when they wrote the Constitution. Of utmost importance in establishing limited government is designing governance to be held closest to the people, and citizens are closest to their elected officials. The foundation of America was predicated on strong state and local governments. The founders believed local government would be best for a civic-led nation.

Most Americans are aware that freedom is a prime virtue of our nation, but few appreciate just how incredible it is that we have preserved freedom so long until they visit other countries. When I speak on college campuses, I often exchange the word *choice* with *freedom* because younger generations seem to relate better to that terminology; they are fairly similar in their meanings and applications in our daily lives. Fundamentally, the divinely inspired Constitution is our key legal document, meant to protect us from infringements upon our freedom by an abusive government. When we look at how dictatorships and abusive governments have destroyed so many lives around the world, it is truly remarkable that we have an 18th century document that still works today as an instrumental legal document for protecting our personal freedoms.

There certainly are variables and individual perspectives that will color how we view our personal level of freedom at any given moment. That is a great thing because it reminds us of the preciousness of this intangible asset, as well as its fragility if we do not safeguard it. Rating our level of freedom is very difficult, but we can get an idea of our commitment to it if we review our nation's priorities related to expenditures on freedom-related services.

Defending freedom requires making it a financial priority, and the United States does just that. In general terms, America spends more than $500 per person each month for professional services that are designed primarily to protect us and our freedoms. This figure is derived from a review of our federal, state, and local expenditures for military, fire, police, and other emergency organizations that work directly to preserve our freedoms, as can be found at www.usgovernmentspending.com. In addition, there are many other support organizations such as legal resources, security, and information technology that also assist in protecting certain aspects of our freedoms. The following are the annual dollars invested in freedom-related services based on 2018 estimates for an approximate US population of 325 million:

- $2,769 for federal (Department of Defense)
- $2,726 for state (state defense and VA-related services)
- $569 for local (police and fire)
- $6,064 combined average per person for all American citizens ($500+/month per person)

Taking on dangerous situations requires a very special type of person, someone who is brave and willing to risk much to save others. Like most Americans, I find it heartwarming to see the gratitude extended to our military, police, and other first responders. Their dedication and sacrifice make it easier for the rest of us to focus on other areas of our lives. America has a rich history of heroes who have been willing to sacrifice much to preserve our freedom. We celebrate and honor them as true role models. Some of these heroes are celebrated on specific days on our calendar:

- Civil rights improvements for our nation on Martin Luther King Day
- Military heroes who gave their lives in defense of our nation on Memorial Day
- The founding fathers of our nation on Independence Day (July 4)
- The workers who comprise the backbone of our nation on Labor Day
- Service members who served in our military on Veterans Day
- Blessings from within our nation on Thanksgiving Day
- The birth of Jesus as the leader of the Christian church on Christmas Day

It takes a very special person to sacrifice much to protect people they may never know personally. These heroes protect us from numerous dangers. I believe the principles that guide many of America's service members in their sacrificial efforts to preserve our freedom are summarized well by the Seven Army Values that guide our US Army. These values are the heartbeat that motivates many of our heroes in taking on extraordinary challenges in the name of freedom.

- Loyalty—Bear true faith and allegiance to the US Constitution, the army, and other soldiers. Be loyal to the nation and its heritage.
- Duty—Fulfill your obligations. Accept responsibility for your own actions and the actions of those entrusted to your care. Find opportunities to improve yourself for the good of the group.

- Respect—Rely on the golden rule. How we consider others reflects on all of us, both personally and as a professional organization.

- Selfless Service—Put the welfare of the nation, the army, and your subordinates before your own. Selfless service leads to organizational teamwork and encompasses discipline, self-control, and faith in the system.

- Honor—Live up to all the army values.

- Integrity—Do what is right, legally and morally. Be willing to do what is right even when no one is looking. It is our "moral compass," an inner voice.

- Personal Courage—Our ability to face fear, danger, or adversity, both physical and moral courage.

In the home of the brave, we are blessed with many courageous people who sacrifice much to keep this nation safe, 24–7, 365 days a year. Life is all about choices, and being able to make our own choices is a special gift. Freedom includes living with the consequences of the decisions we make. It truly is America's friend.

> *The secret of happiness is freedom…And the secret to freedom is courage.*
>
> —Thucydides, ancient Greek historian

★★★≡ QUESTIONS TO PONDER

- When do you feel most free, and how does that empower you to pursue your dreams?

- Who do you think are some of the strongest defenders and detractors of freedom in America today?

- Why do you think freedom can be taken away from us so easily?

4. Prosperity in Abundance

Only societies that embrace open markets, the rule of law, and democracy have seen more people prosper beyond the privileged few.
—Kim Holmes, author and former American diplomat, 2012

A prosperous nation benefits all its citizens, and America is a nation with an abundance of prosperity. With a core belief in capitalism, America has become one of the wealthiest nations on earth. This incredible achievement came through much hard work, combined with a setting that provides genuinely unhindered opportunities for individuals and businesses to provide value in the marketplace. By providing value in the marketplace, America has been able to enjoy many blessings: a higher standard of living, more recreational opportunities than most, greater comforts, safe food and water, and many more amenities that are not as common throughout the rest of the world.

One of the key reasons many immigrants have historically wanted to come to America is that they believed it offered them a greater opportunity to pursue their goals, dreams, and aspirations than their homeland. Every story is different, but many immigrants chose to come to America in its earliest days because they didn't want to be held back in their financial and social mobility by political powers. What was common in that attitude was that most of them did not come to America expecting handouts or an easy road; they came expecting to earn their own way. Citizens come here for the opportunity to pursue their dreams without any guarantee of certain outcomes because opportunities await those willing to work for their rewards.

During our nation's founding years, Thomas Jefferson was asked, "What more is necessary to make us a happy and prosperous people?" His answer? "[A] wise and frugal government, which shall restrain men from injuring one another, shall leave them otherwise free to regulate their own pursuits of industry and improvements, and shall not take from the mouth of labor the bread it has earned."[3] In today's politically correct world, this may come across as fairly harsh, but Jefferson was simply referring to the economic realities of free-market capitalism, in that it worked when people were required to earn their own way. Over time, this works better than forcing others to pay for what they believe they are entitled to without providing any labor or value to the marketplace.

The productivity of US-inspired capitalism, combined with public stability, has beaten every other economic system devised. This system encourages risk-taking, creativity, and healthy competition for anyone who wants to pursue their dream. With the Constitution serving as our rule of law, we have created high levels of political stability and freedom, helping to foster a stronger economy. No authoritarian government has ever succeeded in delivering prosperity to successive generations.

With sufficient prosperity, we have had the financial resources to make a very large impact throughout the world for many noble reasons. For example, since 1800, the world's population has increased six fold, while the United States' gross domestic product (GDP) grew thirty-six-fold. In other words, capitalism has arguably done more to alleviate poverty in the last two hundred years.[4] There is still poverty in the world, but imagine how much worse it would be if not for the rapid expansion of America's GDP.

America's foundation of hard work brought us national prosperity in a relatively short time. The value of hard work and living debt-free is beautifully illustrated by Mike Rowe on his television show *Dirty Jobs*, in which he highlights the importance of some people being willing to take on jobs that most others won't. These jobs may not be glamorous, but devoted people committed to working in these fields are truly the backbone of the American economy. There are always tough, demanding jobs that need to be done with pride. The free market has done a remarkable job of placing value and offering pay for those willing to take on these challenging jobs. Free markets work very well.

America's work ethic has provided us with a strong economic foundation. As we move forward to 2020 and beyond, the virtues of political stability and public support of business enterprises will become even more critical as our world economy comes to be based even more on human capital that can be easily relocated throughout the world. A business-friendly climate will require this country to maintain the following key components, which have historically provided us with strong protection and incentives to prosper within the global economy:

- Emphasize the Constitution as the law of our land over any other ideologies;

- Protect our human capital via clear, consistent legal measures;

- Ensure a healthy business atmosphere backed by political stability; and

- Focus on the positive values that result from free markets.

In addition to America's efficiency in manufacturing and transporting goods around the world, the American way includes strong protective measures for those wishing to create a wide range of intellectual property and services. With legal and public protective measures such as copyrights, patents, trademarks, trade secrets, and publicity rights in place, creative Americans can focus their energies and talents on developing their ideas, knowing they will be protected for a legally specified amount of time.

As the worldwide leader in the production of many goods and services, the United States is blessed with a solid economic foundation. The following are a few examples of how our prosperity provides value for us, as well as future generations:

- An infrastructure that allows us to move people, goods, and services throughout the nation and around the world in an efficient manner;

- Extensive housing, commercial, and recreational properties where we can live, work, and play in comfort;

- Health-care and research services that can cure, eliminate, or slow the growth of numerous illnesses;

- First-class hospitals with high-quality doctors and support staff to keep us healthy;

- First-class military and other emergency personnel who protect us from our enemies;

- Professional performers and athletes to entertain us;

- Extensive communications systems that inform us quickly; and

- Education systems that teach and motivate us to continue discovering new ways to make our country and the world a better place.

Though the current narrative is often that the rich are greedy, the true narrative is that America has a lengthy history of rags-to-riches stories that can serve to motivate us to pursue our dreams to the best of our abilities. Our country provides plenty of opportunity to succeed, as well as to fail. More often than not, we adapt and succeed to some degree. Class mobility is more common in the United States for those of us who are willing to work hard and take on risks to invest in our beliefs than in many countries in Europe, for example. Capitalism can work very well in the real world, with an incredible history of success for many.

Prosperity is nice, but I am a firm believer that wealth in and of itself does not create happiness. For those who are skeptical of this statement, take a moment to research what happens to most people who win a lottery. (The results are not quite what most people expect.) Wealth certainly can buy us comfort and pleasure, but it generally does not buy us happiness or other intangible aspects of fulfillment. One benefit in accumulating wealth is that it allows us to help others in need. Notice that it allows us to identify those who are in need, not a politician who wants to take more of our money to support causes they believe are important (or will help them be re-elected). Personally, I believe most Americans want to be charitable, and I would argue that the return on investment for both the giver and receiver of these individual charitable contributions is much higher than that of those investments made via forced political taxation.

Many Americans are generous in sharing their resources with causes they believe in. We give more and in greater proportion than people anywhere else in the world.[5] The charitable mind-set that resonates in the hearts of many Americans is a beautiful thing to see. In addition to donating our financial resources, more than sixty million Americans give their time to support countless organizations that alleviate many social and physical challenges in our communities. When someone says Americans are selfish, I think the statistics tell a much different story: we are a nation of very strong and generous givers. And, in the end, we all reap rewards from living in a prosperous and charitable country.

We cannot seek achievement for ourselves and forget about progress and prosperity for our community. Our ambitions must be broad enough to include the aspirations and needs of others, for their sakes and for our own.

—Cesar Chavez, American civil rights activist

★★★═══ QUESTIONS TO PONDER

- How has America's abundant prosperity benefited you?
- Why do you think the end results for an overwhelming majority of America's lottery winners turn out so poorly?
- How do you feel about supporting causes you do not believe in with your tax dollars?
- How do you feel about supporting causes you do believe in with your own dollars?

5. The Right to Speak Your Mind

Without freedom of thought, there can be no such thing as wisdom—and no such thing as public liberty without freedom of speech.

—Benjamin Franklin, Founding Father of the United States

Isn't it liberating to know we can speak our minds in a nation that protects our right to free speech? Most of us know about this amendment and cherish it. But just what does it do to protect free speech, and why is it important to us? And, perhaps more importantly, why is this right so guarded in our nation when free speech isn't preserved in so many other nations?

The protection of speech and expression is central to the American political system. It provides us with a direct opportunity to engage in a healthy dialogue about important issues of our day. Free speech enables us to obtain information from a range of sources, formulate our own opinions, make independent decisions, and communicate these perspectives with one another and to our government. Rather than having our government establish and dictate public law based only on its viewpoints, freedom of speech promotes a more citizen-friendly form of law that emerges from a collection of diverse opinions of those most affected by these laws. When freedom of speech is embraced by a nation, citizens are more at liberty to speak openly and honestly, without fear of government restraint.

Operating as a restraint against tyranny, corruption, and ineptitude, freedom of speech provides a system of checks and balances for us to manage our elected officials. For much of world history, governments have played the role of benevolent but firm censor of the opinions of those under its authority. America is different. Our government structure preserves the voices of everyday citizens so their concerns can be heard. We truly have the opportunity to influence the present and future of our nation through our voices.

Open communication allows us to vent our feelings in a productive manner. In a society as diverse as America, providing opportunities for citizens to exercise their opinions offers them a natural and oftentimes productive means of expressing their concerns. It also provides a forum for hearing the opinions of others that might be different, yet might help us reach the best overall solution to a myriad of problems. In America, we have come to accept the wisdom that openness fosters resiliency and that peaceful protests such as those led by Martin Luther King during the 1960s can be an effective measure for displacing more violence and hatred than they trigger.

We embrace freedom of speech for the same reasons we embrace individualism. We enjoy the right to speak defiantly, robustly, and sometimes even irreverently about what is on our minds. Freedom of speech is bonded in unique ways with our identity to think, imagine, and create value and importance within our spheres of influence. Freedom of speech is intimately linked to freedom of thought and our capacity to reason, wonder, hope, and believe in whatever we see in our American dream.

Before looking closer at why the First Amendment is such a significant part of the Constitution, let's take a look at the basics of effective communication. Around the world, most governmental communications have been one-way mandates from a powerful government to its citizens. In a citizen-led nation, the communications between the government and its citizens must be based on, as closely as possible, an open, fair, and transparent process. The most important components of quality communications include:

- Exchange of ideas in a two-way manner, back and forth;

- Communication made in an honest, forthright manner without fear of retaliation;

- Orientation toward problem-solving after matters are analyzed in a realistic manner;

- Recognition by both parties that there are consequences for actions and inactions;

- Respecting the rights of others to speak their minds whether we agree or disagree with the opinions expressed; and

- Some level of trust that can be earned between the parties.

The First Amendment provides a healthy communication tool to be established between citizens and their government. It facilitates healthy and necessary communication with our elected officials.

The First Amendment includes several specific clauses, including the freedom of assembly, freedom of speech, and freedom of the press. These clauses add additional protections to our basic right to free speech.

Freedom of assembly provides the right of individuals to come together and collectively express, promote, pursue, and defend their ideas. It is considered a human right, a political right, and a civil liberty. With this protection, groups are provided the opportunity to get together and peacefully and legally make their views known to others.

Your rights to protest and criticize are almost always permitted within reason. These rights include the right to criticize the government, political advocacy, and advocacy of unpopular ideas. Without free speech protection, we would no longer be a civic-led nation. Some of the core values and benefits of free speech for all Americans include:

- A higher level of self-governance when citizens can fully participate in the political process with access to public information;

- Empowerment to speak out against abuses by those in political power;

- Potential for higher levels of safety by allowing peaceful expression of disagreement; and

- Facilitation of a higher level of individual fulfillment that strongly resonates with the American spirit of freedom.

Our freedom of speech rights are strongly protected in the First Amendment to the Constitution, as well as in many state constitutions. These rights are extensive but not unlimited. For example, categories of speech that are given little or no protection include obscenity, fraud, child pornography, speech integral to illegal conduct or that incites imminent lawless action, and certain regulations related to commercial advertising. Other limits of free speech include:

- copyright, which protects the rights of writers;

- slander, which restricts the use of untruths to harm others; and

- incarceration, which limits the communication rights of persons in prison.

The First Amendment also includes a provision that prevents the government from interfering with the distribution of information and opinions within the press, subject to certain restrictions such as the defamation law. As we learned from what happened in Germany during the 1930s, when the government controlled public disclosures, particularly in the media, this can be dangerous. Government control of information allows the potential for government abuse by creating the type of setting in which there are attempts to motivate citizens to take inappropriate actions and face severe penalties. We have legal provisions to protect us from this abuse.

Isn't it sad the way some people, especially public leaders, just cannot take criticism? When one is a world leader in an authoritarian-style government, one doesn't have to take criticism. More than a dozen nations around the world have specific laws in place that make it an offense punishable by prison time and/or fines simply to criticize their leaders.[5] This should make the citizens of those countries wonder what their leaders may be hiding and help us further understand the value of the opportunities we have to say our piece about own leaders in the free exchange of ideas and opinions, which, in the end, should make for a better community. Once again, the United States was designed much differently.

Freedom of the press protects the right to obtain and publish information or opinions without government censorship or fear of punishment. Censorship occurs when the government examines publications and productions and prohibits the use of material it finds offensive. One unique right given to the press is that the government may not prevent the publication of print material, even when there is reason to believe it could reveal information that may endanger our national security. Other examples of things the government may not do include, for example:

- Pass a law that requires the media to publish information against its will;

- Impose criminal penalties or civil damages on publication of truthful information associated with public concern or even on the dissemination of false information about a public person, except in rare instances;

- Impose taxes on the press that it does not levy on other businesses;

- Compel writers to reveal, in most circumstances, the identities of their sources; and

- Prohibit the press from attending judicial proceedings and informing the public about them afterward.

In addition to protective measures in place by federal law in conjunction with the First Amendment, state and local public bodies also provide some levels of free speech protections for their citizens. Each state and local governmental body has different rules and legal statutes that guide their conduct of public business, but most are covered under some sort of "open meeting law." Each jurisdiction varies in its application, as well as its enforcement, of its open meeting law. Most open meeting laws protect our right to speak our minds with our local elected officials.

- Open meeting laws often restrict a majority of public officials from meeting in private settings to discuss public business to help ensure the debate of public business is conducted in an open forum with some degree of transparency.

- Many open meeting laws require that their political bodies post agendas in advance of their meetings so citizens will know what public decisions are to be discussed and when.

- Open meeting laws require the posting of public votes so the public can be informed of policies enacted and which officials voted for or against the legislation.

America is a much stronger nation as a result of the privilege we have to speak our minds in constructive and even unconstructive ways because it allows our voices to be heard in the development of our nation. This is a tremendous privilege that much of the world is not allowed and a precious reminder that preserving this right helps maintain our future as a citizen-led government.

If the freedom of speech is taken away then dumb and silent we may be led, like sheep to the slaughter.
—George Washington, 1st US President, 1789 to 1797

★★★ QUESTIONS TO PONDER

- What do you think are some possible outcomes of open debates on defining our American values and priorities?

- Why do you think many government leaders like to limit or prevent criticism of their "public actions"?

- How have the rights associated with freedom of speech affected your life?

6. Trusting Citizens with Our Second Amendment

Americans have the right and advantage of being armed—unlike citizens of other countries whose governments are afraid to trust the people with arms.

—James Madison, father of the Constitution

Who do you trust? This is the fundamental question associated with our nation's Second Amendment. In a dangerous world, having the ability to protect ourselves and our loved ones is vital for safety, order, and peace of mind. Many countries in the world have governments that do not trust their citizens and thus restrict their ability to hold and bear arms. Once again, the United States is different. In 1791, the Second Amendment was established to protect citizens against our enemies, both foreign and domestic. It is the only amendment that includes the words "shall not be infringed."

What incredible insight by the writers of the Bill of Rights, who placed their trust in everyday citizens over the possibility of a tyrannical government. How could they have imagined the power and control utilized in dictatorships that would result in the deaths of tens of millions of people in the twentieth century alone just because innocent citizens practiced a religion or spoke about issues government officials did not like? That is exactly what happened in Germany, the Soviet Union, and the People's Republic of China from 1933 on. Fear, terror, and a sense of complete powerlessness surely has been critical to the ability of abusive governments to overpower their own citizens when they deemed them an inferior race or an unworthy social class or classified them as "enemies of the state." This out-of-control power around the world has resulted in far too many atrocities against humanity.

Historically, government power almost always increases without significant restraint by its citizens. Excessive power in the hands of a power-hungry government leads to the creation of rules and laws that make the government stronger while making others more subservient. Our founding fathers recognized that, left unchecked, an out-of-control American government might try to seize power over its citizens by removing their ability to defend themselves. The Second Amendment really is not about guns; it is about power. American citizens are identified in the Second Amendment as the primary stakeholders entrusted with defending themselves, their families, and even their communities against all enemies.

When one assesses what powers US citizens have, the right to keep and bear arms is arguably the strongest, preserving all our other rights. Think about it: Once the right to own firearms is eliminated, taking away other rights becomes much simpler. The Second Amendment is our insurance policy against an abusive government and has protected us for more than two hundred years. It preserves our basic human rights against an overzealous government that attempts to enact restrictions on other basic rights.

The Second Amendment gives citizens the right to be armed and the privilege of defending themselves against tyranny, invasion, and crime. It truly is the defining statement that the rights of citizens are important and to be preserved and not confiscated by a centralized federal government as has happened in other nations over the years. The presence of armed citizens is what keeps the government honest with us.

When citizens are ruled by an abusive government, they become fearful of what they can or cannot do, and their freedoms shrink. Think about it this way: Shouldn't it be difficult for any of us to willingly defer power to someone who is actively seeking to take power from us, including politicians? Having the ability to keep our government honest is fundamental to preserving our freedom to live without fear. Given the tumultuous times in which we live, when politicians are considered some of the least trustworthy people in the country, I certainly appreciate knowing I have this right to protect myself.

Just like all of us, public officials can become frustrated when they do not get what they want. They have the power to enact dangerous laws that will help coerce others to their way. When I entered county politics, believing most elected officials were there to serve the public good, I quickly found that many were actually there, at least to some degree, to control the citizens they were elected to serve. This political mind-set to control rather than serve has occurred at virtually every level of government throughout history. As we review the past, we see the danger of benevolent dictators who prey on docile, indifferent, and gullible citizens who are prepared to accept a set of promises repeated from a bully pulpit. The eventuality of government officials becoming abusive or taking actions that are detrimental to the rights of citizens is almost guaranteed when government power is left unchecked, and the power to resist that evolution is protected by the Second Amendment.

The fundamental purpose of this amendment is to identify who has power and who does not. It is more about people control than gun control. In a world that offers numerous examples of how politicians can become dangerous when we place too much power in their hands, we should be able to identify in whom we place our trust. Do you believe politicians have earned your trust? I find politicians to be one of the more untrustworthy groups of people, and I'm not alone in that opinion. America was founded with an emphasis on a higher level of respect and trust for its citizens than its government, and that has proven to be the right move for a nation focused on freedom and personal rights.

As America confronts the horrifying tragedies associated with mass shootings in public places, many ask our government to step in to remove weapons from citizens. Preventing or minimizing these tragedies will be a security focus for our nation for the foreseeable future, but data often shows that gun bans do not work to deter crime against those intent on breaking the law. In fact, armed citizens taking decisive action against lawbreakers has often resulted in the saving of additional lives. The best way to reduce mass shootings is a complex combination of mental health expertise and advanced security measures, but disarming law-abiding citizens will not solve this serious problem. The bottom line is that lawmakers should be enacting laws that protect as many citizens as possible, not restricting them from having the ability to protect their families from crime.

We are truly the land of the free and the home of the brave when we have the opportunity to defend ourselves against tyrants and lawbreakers who wish to harm us. Keeping our families safe is critical to our future, and the Second Amendment has served as a strong way to preserve our safety.

> *Gun bans don't disarm criminals, gun bans attract them.*
> —Walter Mondale, former vice president of the United States
> (1977–1981)

★★★═══ QUESTIONS TO PONDER

- Why do you think the words "shall not be infringed" were specifically stated only in the Second Amendment?

- What lessons can we learn from the tragic stories of past dictatorships such as Germany from 1933 to 1945, the Soviet Union from 1922 to 1953 and beyond, or the People's Republic of China from 1949 to 1976 and beyond?

- How do you think security technology and mental health treatment considerations can improve our public safety?

7. Civic Support of Our Core Values

Patriotism means to stand by the country. It does not mean to stand by the president or any other public official.
—President Theodore Roosevelt

The growth of political power is relatively consistent throughout world history: eventually, the public sector outgrows itself, and the nation either implodes or starts over. As one of the longest running republic in history, America owes much of its success to the many patriotic citizens who have kept sufficient restraint on our politicians. With numerous concerned citizens keeping a watchful eye over our public sector, America enjoyed a relatively reasonable, limited amount of public-sector growth during most of the nineteenth and twentieth centuries, which helped us prosper mightily in the world economy. America's greatness is defined in many ways by these patriots who have kept our nation's public finances and power in check.

You may be asking, "Why is civic input so important in our nation when it seems that our voice is not heard by so many politicians?" We will address this current-day problem later, but civic input is definitely a critical component. To illustrate its importance, have you ever noticed how your families and neighbors typically care more about your well-being than politicians, who appear to care more about their own reelections? Our founding fathers knew this principle would be important as they prepared the Declaration of Independence and the Bill of Rights that would instill power in the citizenry over the politicians. Human nature is such that we truly care most about those things, as well as those relationships, that most directly affect us. Think about the wisdom and humility exhibited by our founding fathers when they set up a nation that deferred ultimate power to its citizens. This restraint in defining citizens' powers as opposed to those of the government is truly a gift for each of us.

As a civic-led nation, we are fortunate that so many of us care about our nation and its future. Even though we may disagree with one another about some details in the political conversation, active citizen input in our political process builds stronger communities than indifference, especially when civic engagement is grounded in love and respect for the future of our nation. Simply put, America was designed with an emphasis on strong civic leadership that allows us to keep an eye on our public officials. Many generations of Americans have made the nation's dream come true. If the media is considered to be the fourth estate of government, I would argue that civic leadership is our fifth estate, and our most important one for keeping the others accountable to we the people.

What makes civic involvement in the political process so important? From the very beginning, our founding fathers knew from experience that America would not survive as a representative government without civic leaders whose patriotism would oversee the new government's rise above the typical partisan divisions. In another way, political fighting typically leads to division, while respectful citizen patriotism often leads to unity. Benjamin Franklin specifically called for virtuous civic leaders who would be drawn to influencing wise governance as motivated by public interest, not private gain. This type of less biased influence provides a stronger setting for a more virtuous debate that is not watered down by agendas, political spin for political payoff, or politicians focused on power or compensation over serving their constituents. Citizen influence is included in America's governance structure to be powerful and relevant to creating laws that protect the majority.

Civic action that is accomplished outside the constraints and bad influences of money and bureaucracy is crucial for weaving the connections and trust of the public bodies with the voice of the people. With civic involvement comes responsibilities. An effective civic voice is one that is informed and responsible for finding ways to make our communities stronger. Absent this commitment, a free and open society cannot succeed because it will fall into the hands of political powers who may serve for personal gain rather than the public good. Civic leadership is important because it protects the public well-being in many ways:

- Human rights are respected and protected;
- Public expenditures are made with respect for the limited fiscal resources of the taxpayers;
- Individuals' dignity and worth are acknowledged when establishing public laws;
- Peace, safety, and strength are promoted in a manner that protects the way of life of law-abiding citizens;
- The rule of law is observed by our elected officials;
- Rules and laws are established that are sustainable for the public good; and
- Elected officials fulfill their responsibilities with a focus on the greater good, not personal gain.

The public voice of America has been sharpened through many citizens over the years, which has resulted in the development of some amazing communities. These civic-minded individuals and organizations help provide public accountability in various ways, including:

- Bringing campaign promises into focus related to actual public voting records;
- Watching public expenditures, including political thievery and cronyism;
- Requesting appropriate codes of ethics and boundaries on the public sector;

- Identifying violations of public rules and laws made by public officials;

- Building public trust and accountability with those who earn it;

- Informing us how public information will affect us in our daily lives;

- Providing a full circle of accountability to the overall public good; and

- Establishing more realistic considerations of the strengths and weaknesses within the public sector.

A healthy society is essential in preventing abuse or excessive concentration of power by government. Civic leadership reviews important values from a real-life perspective, such as individual rights and responsibilities, concern for the public good, the rule of law, justice, equality, diversity, truth, patriotism, and the separation of powers. Civic leadership works best when these values are evaluated based on important legal documents that guide our nation. For example, the United States Commission on Immigration Reform, in its 1997 Report to Congress (US Commission on Immigration, 1997), strongly recommended attention to the nation's founding documents, saying:

> *Civic instruction in public schools should be rooted in the Declaration of Independence, the Constitution—particularly the Preamble, the Bill of Rights, and the Fourteenth Amendment. Emphasizing the ideals in these documents is in no way a distortion of US history. Instruction in the history of the United States, as a unique engine of human liberty notwithstanding its faults, is an indispensable foundation for solid civics training for all Americans.*

At the core of America's civic strength is a strong, can-do mentality to undertake efforts to help those around us. Civic leadership fundamentally is about living in a manner that embodies the American spirit as independent, productive members of our local communities. Examples of productive civic involvement include:

- **Becoming an independent, responsible member of society.** Adhering voluntarily to self-imposed standards of behavior rather than requiring the imposition of external controls or support of public programs by accepting responsibility for the consequences of one's actions.

- **Respecting individual worth and human dignity.** Respecting others means listening to their opinions, behaving in a civil manner, considering the rights and interests of fellow citizens, and adhering to the principle of majority rule while recognizing the right of the minority to dissent.

- **Participating in civic affairs in a thoughtful and effective manner.** Becoming informed prior to voting or participating in public debate, engaging in civil and reflective discourse, and assuming leadership when appropriate. This includes making an honest assessment of what is best for the public good.

- **Promoting the healthy functioning of political affairs.** Being informed about and attentive to public affairs, learning about and deliberating on constitutional values and principles, monitoring the adherence of political leaders and public agencies to those values and principles, and taking appropriate action if adherence is lacking.

America's civic heroes are everyday citizens who have had a profound impact on our nation. Some have even gone on to become strong public leaders within the political arena. Their intense love of country has shaped it with a powerful allegiance that brings us together in establishing healthy, vibrant communities and states and an unbelievable nation. Throughout the foundational years of our nation, most Americans have truly cared about its well-being, and it shows.

Throughout the first six chapters of this book, we emphasized that America is a civic-led nation. So our real heroes are the people who pull together all these privileges and preserve the great American spirit for their generation, as well as those who follow. America is truly blessed to have had many great leaders who have made profound impacts on our country, including:

- Susan B. Anthony, an early leader of the women's suffrage movement;

- Ralph Waldo Emerson, who promoted the importance of individualism and self-reliance;

- George Gallup, who established polls to help illustrate public views;

- Mark Twain, an unsentimental observer of our national life; and

- Rosa Parks, Thurgood Marshall, Booker T. Washington, Frederick Douglass, Martin Luther King Jr., and many other leaders of the civil rights movement.

When we look at the unbelievable accomplishments of these civic leaders, we have much to be thankful for; they have truly shaped our nation for the better. Some of these leaders' interpersonal qualities, which are important for civic involvement, include:

- Strong loyalty to their beliefs;

- Passion and persistence in seeing positive results that benefit humanity and our nation;

- Strong values and principles that guide their actions;

- An ability to gain public support and persuade elected officials and/or public opinion; and

- A high focus on accountability for achieving positive results and willingness to sacrifice much for their cause.

There have been some excellent role models who have shaped our country's cultural and political values though their persuasive voices. There is a special place in our nation's heritage for our civic heroes; they have shaped this nation in many profound ways and will continue to do so in a citizen-led nation.

> *Expressing our varying political and ideological differences is fundamental to the American experience and essential in finding common ground solutions.*
> —Jason Grumet, founder and president of the Bipartisan Policy Center

★★★═══ QUESTIONS TO PONDER

- What core American values do you cherish the most?

- Who are some civic leaders you respect, and how have they earned your respect?

- How are America's modern-day core values different from those of our earlier years?

- What do you believe is your civic role within your sphere of influence, and what can you do to expand your influence?

III.

Challenges

Forty-four percent of millennials say the idea of the American dream is dead to them. Only 29 percent agree that America is the last, best hope of man on earth.

—Tom Bevan, RealClear Politics, December 08, 2017

With the establishment of a humble country that operates as one nation, under God, with bountiful freedoms and prosperity surrounding it and citizen rights in place to preserve it, America was designed for greatness. And great it was for many years. For more than two hundred years, America was viewed by many around the world as the best hope for man on earth, and many made great sacrifices to bring their families across the ocean to pursue their dreams. So what could go wrong in just a few short decades? When 44 percent of millennials say the idea of the American dream is dead to them, something is seriously wrong.

America is facing a crisis of severe proportions. In some ways, our problems, caused by far too many self-serving politicians and their accomplices, can be difficult to see clearly, but like a ticking time bomb, these problems are deadly. Just as in 1964, when the US surgeon general determined that cigarettes were a main contributor to several diseases and death, I believe when we look back on the current dismantling of America from within, this issue of the unhealthy growth in government will also be defined as a dangerous, deadly disease. We are getting very close to living in a once-vibrant nation that may no longer be fixable, which is a sobering thought.

Other problems facing us today, such as our cultural divide, are more visible. It is easy to see riots and protests since they are covered regularly in the media. We *see* a growing lack of respect for our nation's identity by many public personalities. We *feel* the tension that is dividing a once-united America in so many ugly ways. Those fighting our foundational American culture bring these grievances to our politicians, and we become a politicized nation where we insidiously keep asking politicians to solve more and more problems, even though we do not like the results. We keep thinking our political party is right and the other is wrong, without ever looking at what is best for America, no matter the political affiliation. And through these problems, our frustrations increase and our patience decreases as our national identity evolves into something that historically has not worked.

No matter how one looks at the situation, it is not a pretty sight, and the results are devastating, as far too many of us no longer believe that America is the last best hope of man on earth or that our nation will be better off for the next generation. The problem is very wide and very deep; this problem goes far beyond our federal government to political problems that exist at virtually every level throughout this nation. And those who have stolen the power from we the people do not want to give it back. America has let its guard down, and the political elites and their accomplices have taken control of our nation in many ways. And the results are not good, no matter what barometer one uses to define success or failure.

In today's political dialogue, much of our nation focuses its attention on whether any particular president is doing a good or bad job. Though these conversations can be interesting or frustrating, they generally do not address the depth of the overall problem. When looking at the overall mess our nation is in, our president is only capable of fixing a small percentage of the problems. There are so many other levels of government that control us, from nation to state to localities. We the people technically have a larger voice in our nation's governance than any politician if we can just regain that lost power and privilege.

America's internal fighting is eating away at the foundation of a powerful nation. A nation built on rugged independence is being replaced by a growing desire to have government take care of more and more of our problems, even as it goes deeper and deeper into debt. We are at a sad time when it is considered politically incorrect to stand strong for the foundational values that established America as an exceptional place to live, work and play, with opportunities for all. Political and cultural pressures to disregard the validity and applicability of our foundational values represent a serious challenge to our future.

The centerpiece of this internal struggle in our culture is the political arena, where our elected officials have been pressured to focus more on social rights and modifying America's traditional values to fit a minority voice that is screaming loudly for change. Any organization should always listen for ways to improve, but when the voice of a small segment is given more attention than that of the majority, it is time to assess the role of those institutions. There are certainly some social issues that need to be debated in circles, but this expanded focus has taken away attention from important public infrastructure needs such as roads and defense. Many are growing weary of the daily narrative that makes it acceptable to be blatantly critical of America's traditional values without offering positive alternatives.

Knowing how to stand up and defend our values will continue to grow in importance until the greatness of America can overcome the negativity associated with a minor yet large and growing voice in America's culture. Let's take a look at some of these ongoing challenges facing America in 2018.

★★★══ QUESTIONS TO PONDER

- What challenges to the American way bother you the most?

- What does the ideal American dream look like to you, and what is stopping us from making that dream possible?

- Have you ever been in a political discussion where you felt helpless or frustrated? What frustrated you the most?

8. American Values Under Attack

Our government leaders have made many mistakes in the past when they have lost sight of the sacred American values rooted in the Declaration of Independence and the Constitution. We are at the brink of even graver mistakes and assaults on these values.

—Samuel Dash, chief counsel for the Senate Watergate Committee, 1973

The American way is under attack by numerous powers within our own borders. These attacks are relentless, focused on undermining America's core values, especially freedom, liberty, capitalism, independence, and even the moral validity of our laws. The nation is losing its' identify as strong and self-sustaining. But who is behind these attacks, and what are their goals?

Defining who is behind the attacks on America and their motivation to disrupt and/or significantly modify the American way can be difficult because there are obviously many perspectives to consider. Though it can be difficult to completely identify these motivations, we must make some educated assessments if we are going to understand what is needed to solve the serious challenges facing America's cultural and political divide today. I'm sure each reader has their own opinion on why these attacks are happening, who is behind them, and how severely they are affecting our nation. I believe the primary objective of many attacking the American way today is to redefine the American way into 'a new and better way' by creating division and confusion about the importance and relevance of our traditional values.

The specific qualities generated by "a new and better way" are rarely discussed in depth other than as a general Utopian idea that a more socialist nation will be better than the traditional American way (even though history shows much different results in other socialist nations). I believe the motives behind this movement are often based on a lack of understanding and appreciation of the blessings we already have. In many ways, we have become complacent or indifferent, grasping the abundance we have all around us without sensing any urgencies. No matter what is driving them, few disagree that our values are under relentless attack, coming from many angles. Let's take a look at some of them.

Redefining our past: The attacks often begin with an effort to destroy our history and our heritage. This has become much easier to do during the rapid expansion of social media, on which distortions of reality become more and more common. Efforts to modify or erase history are dangerous to any civilized nation, especially one as successful as America has been. The American dream is easier to destroy for future generations when the past is changed to tell a different story. Modifying our heritage destroys our identity because if one can redefine the past, it becomes easier to change the future. For example, efforts to degrade or remove public monuments or displays, no matter how good or bad they may be, distort the reality of our national identity.

A growing indifference to embracing American values: With reduced focus on the civic heritage and blessings provided to citizens of our nation, we have less understanding and appreciation of how the American way provides value in our personal lives. Sometimes we don't know what we have until we lose it, making it difficult for some to comprehend the privileges, as well as the responsibilities, that come with living the American dream.

Living beyond our means: America's debt has skyrocketed over the past forty years. We spend well beyond our means. And when we do, it becomes more common to ask others to help pay our bills. This results in class warfare, under the premise that it is only fair for those who make more than we do to pay our personal bills through forced taxation. This has resulted in numerous social and economic plights that hinder America's stability in many ways. Unfortunately, the school of hard knocks has been replaced with a mind-set of doing what feels best now and worrying about the consequences later.

Changing from equal opportunity to equal outcome: When we live beyond our means, it becomes easier to be attracted to ideas in which other people are forced to pay our bills. This movement has become a frontal assault on both individual responsibility and the capitalist market system. This entitlement mentality is not healthy; it fosters the idea of taking from others as the primary economic tool of the new American way, instead of sweat equity to receive compensation for an honest day's work. Americans used to look up to successful people as role models. In today's reverse perspective, they are now frequently labeled "the greedy rich." With these attacks on success, we go into a vicious cycle of changing our societal identity of what works well and what does not.

Replacing private responsibility with public responsibility: Individual responsibility has been replaced with public responsibility, with politicians more than willing to grow their power. It has become far too easy to ask politicians to pick up the slack for whatever problem we have in our communities because they place restraints on how they spend other people's money, but that option has resulted in a $21 trillion national debt and little progress in solving social problems. A nation that once lived within its means has now gone broke playing "Mr. Nice Guy" with other people's money. There are many who still believe the public sector is better than the private sector in solving our complex problems, even though there is minimal evidence to support this belief.

Replacing moral values with relativism and intolerance: Americans who stand up against wrongs and injustices are frequently referred to as intolerant, bigoted, or racist, and those views are considered unacceptable as part of the new American way. We have replaced our moral compass of absolute right and wrong with moral relativism, which redefines right and wrong based on subjective interpretations applicable to each individual. This is challenging and frankly unfair for law-abiding Americans. Every nation creates laws based on some form of acceptable behavior. Modifying our principles to meet ever-changing politically correct terms results in less clarity in defining what behavior our society condones. Examples of attacks on morality and many of our religious traditions include:

- A twisted definition of separation of church and state not found in our Constitution;

- Adding protected religious status for new religious organizations that are contrary to traditional forms of religion associated with God, such as atheism, Wicca, etc.;

- Constant promoting of immoral behavior as the new normal and demanding that the public should pay the higher societal costs associated with these actions (e.g., public programs to provide drug users with safe needles to inject their drugs);

- Creation of a double standard in legal definitions, such as referring to an unborn baby as a fetus if a mother wants to abort him or her, then changing the status of that unborn baby to a child if the mother is killed in an accident; and

- Continued erosion of our godly heritage and moral principles as secularists and eager politicians' push to replace God with government as the main doctrine guiding our nation.

The rule of law no longer applies in many situations: When a society becomes lax in enforcing its laws, it crumbles, and America is doing just that. The Constitution is our law of the land, yet very few public officials understand it, refer to it, or set laws that follow it. Behavior clearly defined as right and wrong via our legal system has been modified or eliminated and replaced with political actions that justify illegal activities in support of political appeasements.

Public officials abusing power to address private grievances and endorsing inappropriate behavior: It has become more common for public officials to use their pulpits to voice personal concerns and endorse inappropriate or illegal behavior. For example, several members of the Ann Arbor, Michigan, city council chose to kneel before the US flag during the reciting of the Pledge of Allegiance before one of their council meetings.[6]

The job of a city council member at an official public meeting is to take care of the business of the city in accordance with the oath to uphold the Constitution, not to overtly insert their personal opinions about any given subject.

Public funds used for private profit: Backroom deals benefit the politician and hurt the taxpayer; there is a reason the deals are not made in public. For example, the Minneapolis City Council recently voted to remove $140,000 from their previously approved 2018 public budget so they could give themselves $10,000 raises.[7] This vote was taken without any discussion, which would lead most reasonable people to conclude that this agreement had been previously made, illegally, behind closed doors. Backroom deals cost the public much. Politicians are openly disregarding the concerns and voices of the people as their power structure keeps information internal, and they far too often no longer represent the voice of the people.

Voice of respect replaced with voice of complaint: As a result of these attacks on the American way, the loudest voice in America has gone from one of admiration and respect for the pillars on which we stand to one of constant complaint that there must be something better. The constant blame game in America has diminished the hope for the future in many. Examples of disrespect toward our symbolic heritage include removing historical monuments and defiantly kneeling during the singing of our national anthem.

Constraints on our freedom of speech: Our freedom of speech is whittled down each and every day, especially in many of our public schools, where one would think students should be allowed to speak their minds freely. The voice of free will has been reversed into a discussion of what our government will let us do instead of the original intention of allowing us to be free to speak our minds to our government. This is very dangerous for any nation that values free speech.

It has become increasingly more acceptable under the guise of modernization to beat up on the traditional values that have guided America for more than two hundred years. With the rapid increase in the use of social media, the bashing of America with limited truth or even outright lies with minimal accountability has become all too common. The problem is that complaining is relatively easy to do, but real progress can only be made when solutions are offered. Americans may disagree on the best remedy for our problems, but it is more beneficial to identify a problem and solution in the same discussion. Today's America seems to have an abundance of problems with few realistic solutions to overcome the challenges facing our nation.

> *In a free society, government reflects the soul of its people. If people want change at the top, they will have to live in different ways. Our major social problems are not the cause of our decadence. They are a reflection of it.*
>
> —Cal Thomas, syndicated columnist

★★★═══ QUESTIONS TO PONDER

- What traditional American values are being attacked the most in your community and in other parts of our nation?

- How is the voice of mainstream America being drowned out by fringe groups?

- Why do you think disgruntled Americans are demanding a new American way?

9. Who Can We Trust?

American faith in government is in free fall. In the late 1950s and early 1960s, more than 70 percent of Americans believed that government could be trusted "always or most of the time," compared with just 19 percent who said the same at the end of 2015.

—Jeffrey D. Sachs, "Restoring Civic Virtue in America,"
Boston Globe, December 4, 2016

Who do you trust? In today's world, this question is becoming more and more important, and unfortunately, the typical American is finding fewer sources of reliable, unbiased information. Does it seem as if telling the truth is important in our personal lives, where families and businesses rely on some level of accountability and respect for one another, while in the political world, lies and deceit happen far too frequently? Why do our elected officials and their accomplices have such a different level of respect and accountability than hardworking families? And how does this damage the sustainability of our nation?

According to Jeffrey Sachs's article, the direst threat American society faces today is the collapse of civic virtue. He defines civic virtue as "honesty and trust that enables the country to function as a decent, forward-looking, optimistic nation." The defining characteristic of our society today is that Americans trust neither their politicians nor their accomplices. What a sad commentary on our great nation, but how can we argue with his point when we struggle to find any semblance of truth in the news of our day? Our once-optimistic nation is being smothered in lies and deceit.

One would think that a respectable government would strive to protect its citizens by informing us of the risks and dangers we face. This approach goes hand in hand with the primary public-office task of overseeing the protection of citizens. Unfortunately, that style of political talk does not work well for reelection, so it is rarely used. Far too many of our politicians have inserted a self-protective measure that limits how real and forthright they are with their constituents. That is why political spin is so common. Politicians are surrounded by a bubble of accomplices and are rarely truly connected with the genuine heartbeat of their constituents. But how are they able to get away with so many lies when constituents want to know what is going on with *their* government? Here are a few of the reasons this happens:

- Reality is perceived much differently through the eyes of politicians and their accomplices than through those of the average hardworking American;

- As a result, politicians have become highly skilled in providing half-true answers to many questions that fit their narrative;

- Political deliberation often takes place during working hours, and these stories are later told to us with bias and spin that make it difficult to capture the facts and the rationale behind the facts;

- Reliable information takes time and effort to find; and

- Politicians frequently blame others publicly, then make deals behind closed doors. (We hear the blame, but we do not see the private contradictory action.)

The end result is that many give up trying to identify the truth in far too many political situations.

In addition to the political spin, we live in a lightning-fast society where few of us are able to take the time to slow down and assess our nation's problems. I have spoken to many good-hearted Americans who care deeply about our future, but their busy schedules only allow seconds or minutes of each day for politics. Reading or listening to public discourse takes energy and active discernment to identify biases and slants. That calls for hours of undivided attention to look at issues more accurately and see through clouds of deceit.

Recognizing that many Americans have very limited time for active civic engagement, politicians and their accomplices have become adept at telling their version of the story. Here are several examples of lies and spin commonly found in today's political news:

- Leaving out or modifying the primary premise(s) behind the reason a vote took place;

- Releasing an exaggerated amount of positive news to coincide with reelection efforts;

- Using political jargon the average citizen may not understand;

- Asking others to smear an opponent with false allegations; and

- Strong public relations messaging that stimulates emotional appeals to spend more public dollars while minimizing associated costs.

Some politicians and their accomplices have become adept at spoon-feeding us their stories with a primary focus on helping their reelection. They create fairy-tale stories that everything is all right or that the problems are not as bad as they might appear. Their manipulation of the facts and backroom deals are designed to maintain their own power structures by controlling information and dissemination. (This is very dangerous, as we know from Germany in the 1930s.) After seeing the negative effects of backroom deals for four years in my county, I came to the conclusion that backroom deals served no public purpose, though they did serve the political purpose of benefitting the politicians and the insiders at the expense of the people they were elected to serve. It makes you wonder why public decisions are made almost entirely in private. What are they hiding from us?

Political lies and spin have been happening for a long time, but the intensity sure seems to have expanded with the growth of the public sector over the past forty years. Helping spin the yarn are accomplices who spin the truth to fit their own agenda. This happens everywhere, and I will illustrate an example of something I have shared with audiences around the nation these past few years.

Just a few months after I began serving as county commissioner for Isanti County, Minnesota, we had an important vote on our comprehensive plan. I believed the plan had some major flaws, and I prepared my notes so I could explain why I was not going to vote in favor of it. We had a fairly large crowd of concerned citizens at the meeting, and I vividly remember watching many people nodding in agreement when I expressed my reasons. The comprehensive plan was passed on a four-to-one vote with my opposition, and I thought that was just politics where you win some and you lose some. End of story, or so I thought.

A week later, a scathing letter to the editor appeared in our local newspaper entitled "Commissioner Duff off to a rocky start."[8] The writer went on to say that Commissioner Duff had better learn how to work with this board and learn to speak the "Isanti County tone." The letter was quite harsh and seemed really out of balance with the actual situation. I'd spoken calmly about my opposition to the plan and believed the audience seemed to agree with my concerns. Unsure how this person could have come to his conclusion, I called him and thanked him for speaking to me. When I asked where in the audience he was sitting at the meeting when he had heard me being unreasonable or disrespectful, he freely admitted he was not there. I later found out he was the campaign manager of one of the other commissioners, and this was an attempt by the political insiders to discredit my voice.

I thought it was best for the residents of our county to hear the other side of the story. I wrote a response letter to the editor, in which I referenced the point about my tone from a person who admitted he was not there to hear it.[9] I added that going forward, because of this false allegation, I would be recording our meetings so the public could hear for themselves the words, as well as the tone, of everyone who spoke. This was when I found out just how much politicians hate to be held accountable for their actions. One of the other commissioners even asked our attorney if it was legal for me to record our public meetings. In sum, politicians often want to revise their stories, even if it means lying or spinning events to suit themselves. And if elected officials do not want to confront the reality of a situation themselves, they are not afraid to have their accomplices work to revise a story to their liking.

This kind of nonsense happens every day in American politics, and it can be very tiring to get to the bottom of things, to the genuine truth of political narratives. Just look at the commentary that goes on about the president every single day; it is easy to see why we tune out. The truth may set us free, but we have a hard time finding it in American politics.

At the heart of political communication is the fact that it takes discernment to identify biases and slants, and average Americans simply do not have enough time to fully dissect the news they receive in a manner that helps them best discern the truth of any reporting. America is saturated with an extreme bias of over reporting problems and underreporting successes. There are four types of problems commonly found in reporting of political and cultural stories:

- Over reporting problems to sell news and neglecting the productive aspects of a successful nation;

- Over reporting political successes to help support political favorites in hopes of gaining favors;

- A strong emphasis on telling the underdog's story (the minority voice), which is nice but can often distort the voice of the majority views on numerous subjects; and

- Naive media who do not understand how much their personal biases affect their ability to provide impartial reporting.

For those who have never been on television, it can be quite an interesting experience, especially in the crazy world of politics. You never know just how a reporter is going to piece together stories, and typically their biases are clear once you understand the talking points they use, as well as the talking points they do not allow on the air. Sometimes these stories are spun without intention due to strong political biases. Other times, they can be deliberately "recreated" to tell the story the journalists want to tell.

Another form of political spin comes frequently from overly biased citizens. You know, someone who says everything President Trump does is right or wrong or who holds completely different standards for different political parties, rather than making an honest assessment. Passionate civic engagement is encouraging to see, but we need citizens who can recognize that we can often get caught up in tunnel vision, seeing politics only through our own unique biases.

In sum, America struggles to function as an orderly nation due to lies, deceit, and a general lack of accountability that destroys our overall public trust. Trust is critical to any worthy relationship, and politicians have very little of it from most of the American public. We no longer respect our elected officials and, by default, the nation they represent. Some of the biggest problems this has created include:

- Making it difficult for us to see hope for a better future because so many false narratives create cultural divisions throughout our nation;

- Making it challenging for us to be effective civic participants because we struggle to obtain reliable information to help us form better opinions and dialogue;

- Increasing our fear of speaking in opposition when we see public backlash against those speaking out against unreasonable political decisions;

- Diverting attention from solving real problems and creating real value in the marketplace as we spend time separating fake news from the truth;

- Discouraging many good people from even contemplating serving in elected office, with dirty, slanderous politics becoming the norm in far too many circles; and

- Making us cynical about our ability to make a positive difference in a public sector that has distanced itself from our real issues.

The blueprint for a successful America was in place for more than two hundred years, but a new way has been brought to us through many lies and deceptions, making it virtually impossible for everyday Americans to place any trust in their processes. When this happens, the results include civic frustration and lost hope. As I learned in military officer schooling, trust must be earned, and our trust in our public officials is essentially nonexistent at so many levels, a truly sad state of affairs for our great nation.

> *I read the paper every day and the Bible every day; that way I know what both sides are up to.*

—Zig Ziglar, author, salesman, and motivational speaker

★★★═══ QUESTIONS TO PONDER

- Who do you trust?

- Why do you think politicians have a difficult time earning our trust?

- What are some of the most blatant biases you see in today's media?

- How do you determine what is true as you evaluate political electability?

10. Misunderstanding the Priorities of Politicians

Politicians as a class are dangerous, that people who are seeking power over us are not, by definition, our friends.
—James Bovard, author, American Libertarian

As in all professions, there are good politicians as well as bad. It is difficult to generalize and stereotype all politicians as bad because there are so many exceptions. However, we are at a time in US history when our disdain for and lack of trust in our politicians is very high, so we need to ask why. Why are we so disappointed in so many of our elected officials?

In many ways, politicians have earned their poor reputations through their actions, which are often short on honor, integrity, and respect for their constituents. On the other hand, we get what we vote for, so it seems appropriate that we evaluate a citizen's typical understanding of the role of a politician and why we vote the way we do. What are our expectations of our elected officials? When so many citizens know we have serious problems but want to feel good about their communities, politicians have a vested interest in telling us everything will be all right if we vote for them. Typically, when we ask our politicians to solve more problems, we set up minimal expectations of defining limits and living within our means, as most citizens do in real life.

An overwhelming majority of Americans vote based on which political candidate they believe cares most about them and the issues that matter to them. Some want to believe their elected officials can be their friends. Although this may be viewed as normal, this mind-set usually sets us up for disappointment. While freedom can be our friend, as discussed earlier, viewing politicians that way can be dangerous. Politicians are supposed to serve in an impartial manner, as public trustees, while managing limited public resources. The hard reality is that the average taxpayer does not make the list of top five friends for the average politician because their relationships are almost always prioritized in an order that looks something like this:

- Commitment to self: acquire power and stay in power through reelections;

- Commitment to party and/or other politicians: expand their influence for their own benefit;

- Commitment to growing the organization they represent: socialize with their employees much more than with taxpayers;

- Commitment to accomplices: stay in power with the aid of individuals and organizations who disseminate information in helpful ways;

- Commitment to contributors: reward those who pay to play; if you don't pay, your voice matters little; and

- Commitment to campaign rhetoric: attract voters by making them think you care about them, especially at election time.

In sum, politicians care most about their own power and then your vote. When we mistakenly believe they care about us and the issues we think are important, we are setting ourselves up for disappointment. And that's what is happening far too often as the distance between voters and politicians widens throughout so many political jurisdictions around the nation.

All in all, most people will appreciate truth more than flattery, and that is the problem. Most politicians are highly skilled at flattering their audience, while in the end, their results almost never satisfy their electorate and we become frustrated that our voices aren't being heard or respected. The painful truth is that we have a mess on our hands in the political arena, and no one politician can fix it. The significant disconnect between political promises and the realities citizens face in their personal, economic, and social situations starts early in the game, when we misunderstand the true priorities of our politicians. Americans stubbornly continue to believe politicians will fix problems when there is minimal evidence they can.

To further illustrate how little the typical politician cares about our well-being, let's take a quick look at the American welfare system. Most of us would agree that providing a safety net for those facing hardship is the right thing to do. However, isn't it fairly easy to say that the American welfare system has gone too far in helping those in need to a level that removes any reasonable expectation of personal responsibility? There are many who blatantly abuse the welfare system, and it costs us all.

Genuine care for our well-being includes encouragement to take care of ourselves, not facilitating dependence on an impersonal helping hand. When one looks at public programs from this perspective, they can be seen as bureaucratic, impersonal, and frankly dehumanizing. The person receiving the welfare check is treated like a statistic or a problem, not a human being with potential. This goes against the mind-set of our nation, in which we are all treated with dignity, with full capability of pursuing happiness without the government holding us back. Hardship support was provided quite well for many decades by more vested stakeholders such as our families, churches, and nonprofits, but these have been replaced in the past several decades by an impersonal government, and the long-term results are hurting more than helping.

As discussed earlier, an overwhelming majority of public decisions are made by our politicians in private. These decisions often conceal their real intent from the people they are intended to serve, and they benefit the politicians as they prepare for reelection. As part of this process, politicians spend an overwhelming amount of time campaigning for their next election and significantly less time doing the actual work of governance. When a politician tells you they spend X number of hours per week on their job, your response should be, "How many of those hours are spent benefiting your constituents versus helping yourself?" In my observation, I would estimate that most politicians spend more than half their time in office working toward reelection or helping others expand their power within the system. With high salaries in place for many elected officials, we are essentially paying them to constantly campaign and become career politicians. Citizens used to benefit from strong elected officials serving their best interests, but that has transitioned significantly into many benefits for the politician at a cost to the people they are elected to serve.

The American political system has been modified by insiders to foster reelection in many ways that make it difficult for grassroots efforts to overcome the insidious political monstrosity. The evolution of political office has gone from one of honored privilege to serve the public to building and maintaining power and influence over the people, not working to serve them. Their priority is election and reelection, not serving their constituents. Career politicians have the reelection game down, and we the people get left behind.

In addition, cronyism is truly alive, as we now have many political organizations that believe it is their responsibility to force taxation so they can give money to their favorite charities and hence, grow their power and sphere of influence. As an example of politicians promoting themselves and abusing their public office, the following is an excerpt from a letter to the editor from one of our county commissioners that has received much discussion in our local area.

Isanti County Commission on Aging appreciates support

Dear Editor:

We, the undersigned members of the Isanti County Commission on Aging (ICCOA), take this opportunity to express our "Thank You" to the commissioners of Isanti County for their past and continued financial support of the Senior Enrichment Center (SAC's). Your support enables us to make a positive impact on the lives of seniors and the community, itself, via our programs and activities and operations of the Friendship Cafe.

Isanti County Commission on Aging
Susan Morris, Chair
Lewis Leasure, Vice Chair

Source: Isanti County News, March 30, 2018

This letter was written by a public official essentially thanking herself for donating public funds to a charitable organization she chairs. (Susan Morris serves as an Isanti County commissioner as well as chair of the nonprofit group Isanti County Commission on Aging.) Our local community discussed this letter and how this was at the heart of what was wrong with politics today. First, they could not believe the public relations grandstanding of a politician thanking herself for giving public funds to a charity she chairs. Second, they questioned why there were no ethical standards to prevent an obvious conflict of interest in the distribution of funds. And lastly, they were concerned at the lack of understanding that the funder of this charity was the taxpayer, not the politician.

Most citizens understand this conflict of interest and grow frustrated that politicians continue with this type of reckless behavior. Most further understand that the primary concern of the politician was promoting herself for reelection and not the charity. Unfortunately, many politicians believe our first allegiance is to them and their control, when the role of an elected official is to protect the safety and vitality of the citizens they are elected to serve. When their job expands beyond that and political mischief is allowed, our public funds become a playground for the out-of-control political elites who are eager to spend more and more of our hard-earned money for their favorite charities. When politicians treat our tax dollars as if they are theirs, we get frustrated, and our faith in our government continues to disintegrate.

The first priority of our politicians has changed from managing public programs with limited fiscal resources to an endless expansion of new ideas on how to solve more and more problems at more and more cost to the tax payer. This revised priority ranking has resulted in severe frustration in the taxpayers of our nation and continuing social and economic decay. Until more Americans recognize that politicians are there to serve many needs before those of their constituents, starting with themselves, we will continue to have a frustrated and divided America.

> *People are fed up with the career politicians who created this*
> *mess or failed to prevent it and neither was acceptable, and*

the only way we could change that was by sending a different type of person to Washington.
—Ted Yoho (R), US representative, Florida

★★★═══ QUESTIONS TO PONDER

- Why do you think politicians care more about the opinions and interests of other politicians than those of the people they are elected to serve?

- Do you think politicians make decisions based more on principles or personalities?

- What do you think should be the primary responsibilities of an elected official in today's American culture?

11. The Unhealthy Expansion of Public Gluttony

There's a whole generation growing up thinking...the government exists to care for them.
—Dave Ramsey, American businessman, author and
radio host

In a nation founded on independence, just how much government do we really need? The cost of government has gone from minimal during our first 150 to 200 years to nearly half our nation's gross domestic product (GDP). And it surrounds us everywhere; for example, as we look at the fine print of our hotel and restaurant bills, we often see taxes amounting to 25, 40, and even as high as 50 percent of the value of the service we just bought. When will it stop? Based on my experience inside the political backrooms, this gluttony has no end in sight; politicians truly love to spend other people's money. How bad is this unhealthy expansion of our public gluttony? Just consider this startling fact:

> Americans will pay an estimated $4 trillion in taxes in 2012: $152 billion *more* than we spend on housing, food, and clothing, *combined.*[10]

America spends more on taxes than on the three most basic parts of living (food, shelter, and clothing). Wow! When a nation forces its citizens to pay more in taxes than their basic living needs, it may be time to reconsider our collective priorities. Despite our excessive taxation, we have little to show for it other than a $21 trillion debt and many frustrated citizens. Isn't it sad that one of the most prosperous nations in the history of the world is going broke because it spends well beyond its means?

Our politicians have an addiction to other people's money (OPM). When I speak with concerned citizens about the problems in politics, we may disagree about which party is best suited to address our problems, but one thing that is almost always agreed upon is that we simply have too much taxation, especially our personal share of this burden. The average person truly wants less taxation, yet it is so simple to tax others we do not know so that our pet projects and programs can continue. The sad part of this story is that we have a completely unrealistic situation on our hands, in which an overwhelming majority of politicians want more government to pay for more utopian projects, and we are truly going broke trying to pay for this undefined fantasyland.

Exacerbating the problem is the fact that once a public program is set up and funded, it is virtually impossible to take it away. Occasionally, some public officials may insert some form of accountability and assessment of return on investment, but rarely are government programs streamlined to fit within defined limits. And for those politicians who try to curtail this spending, their duration of power in office is usually short; career politicians and their accomplices who want more power will team up to push those who want reasonable limits to the streets because they are not allowed to play in the ever-expanding public arena. It is very rare to find a public organization that reduces its expenditures, completely the opposite of most of our family or business budgets, in which cuts are a regular occurrence. So why can't our politicians live within their means?

History repeats itself, often. We must learn from it, or we will keep repeating it. Unfortunately, America is going down the same path that has destroyed many nations before us. And, in the political world, the outcome for governments that grow beyond their means is unbelievably bad; it always ends up with public abuses against the rights of its people. These are just the basics of history, and it is amazing how virtually every nation moves in that direction, with those in power believing they are entitled to more and more power under the misleading premise of "helping their citizens" with other people's money. What they fail to realize is that government is not intended to help people, but rather to protect them from others, including themselves.

Part of the problem is systemic in our instant-gratification society, where we expect so much and want it now, instead of planning our expenditures and patiently waiting to make purchases when we have the funds to do so in a responsible manner. Throughout America today, our public gluttony begins at home, then expands as we ask our government to help fix more and more of our problems—with other people's money. And based on my experience as a county commissioner, there is very little reluctance from our government to accommodate those expanding requests. Unfortunately, these requests are often accommodated with minimal respect or concern for the taxpayers footing the bill. It's as if we have an abundance of moochers electing thieves to steal from the economic producers of our society.

When American citizens abandon their responsibility to cope with their own problems with their own resources, aided at times by compassionate assistance from friends and family when necessary, Americans frequently respond with, "The government will take care of it. That's why I pay taxes."

Let's take a moment to consider the implications of this attitude. Let's say Paul wants a social program that will pay him benefits he believes he is entitled to, and he wants Peter to pay for this by the government increasing Peter's taxes. If Paul can persuade enough politicians to authorize the program and increase taxes to fund it, he can receive a subsidy with a reasonably clear conscience since it is all "legal." Once that precedent is set, Paul is likely to ask for more and more funds via higher taxation until Peter's resources are exhausted. (Because public entitlement programs very rarely provide true fixes to our problems, it becomes easy for Paul to claim he needs even more help.) Takers have few limits, and unfortunately, the givers in the story, the politicians, have few limits either.

In the scenario above, if Paul were to take money from an unwilling Peter without the complicity of the government, Paul would face fines and imprisonment as a criminal. In fact, most Pauls' do not make these unreasonable requests in private-sector settings due to the moral restraints of our consciences (as well as fear of going to prison). So why should it be any different for us to do the same thing with our politicians under the guise of compassion or it only being fair? Far too many of our public programs have become crutches that hinder the human spirit rather than motivating those recipients to an enhanced self-sufficiency and self-actualization.

The tragedy of this story is that once the confiscation of other people's money through the power of taxation is set in motion, robbing Peter to pay for Paul's problems inevitably increases the growth of government and erodes the conscientious responsibility of its people. In the past, this vicious cycle has almost always led to moral anarchy and ended in political dictatorship where our freedoms erode. We then pay for a much larger government via law enforcement and social programs to cope with the resulting social problems. As William Penn once stated: "Those people who are not governed by God will be ruled by tyrants." And that is where America sadly sits in 2018.

Some say it is only "fair" to tax others to help make things equal throughout our economy. According to Milton Friedman, an American economist, dangerous things happen when you only aim at equality by giving some people the right to take things from others. What ultimately happens when society aims at equality is that A and B decide what C shall do for D (and A and B take a commission fee along the way), and we all suffer.[11] The premise of capitalism is that we are motivated to work harder when we can be fairly compensated for our efforts. This order of producing the best return on our investments, which produces the best value, works something like this:

- Highest motivation is personal expenditures for personal use;

- Second-best motivation is personal expenditures for others' use (buying for a friend);

- Third-highest level of motivation is using others' assets for our own personal use; and

- The worst motivation is using others' assets to redistribute to others. (There simply is no reason to bargain shop or provide genuine value.)

Before thinking Americans are heartless and have little compassion for those in need, it would be wise to review our voluntary giving as a nation. Americans by and large love to give, especially when they can control their giving to those needs they personally believe in. Americans give more and in greater proportion than anyone else in the world.[12] Nothing is more indicative of a healthy civic mind-set than one who recognizes the duty to help others voluntarily. We are a compassionate society, and that is defined by our philanthropy, not forced taxation. Forced taxation is based on greed and gluttony, spending other people's money, while true compassion sits with the many generous Americans who give freely of their time and resources for many notable causes. Unfortunately, far too many Americans believe forced taxation is more compassionate than freely giving to charities as desired by the individual.

Absolute power corrupts absolutely, and public gluttony begins early in the political process, from campaign donations to lifelong pay to post-service benefits for career politicians. Our public gluttony is destroying a once-mighty nation. America is living on borrowed time, as well as an overloaded credit card. For one of the most prosperous nations in the world, that is truly sad.

> *You cannot help the poor man by destroying the rich. You cannot keep out of trouble by spending more than your income. You cannot further the brotherhood of man by inciting class hatred. You cannot establish security on borrowed money. You cannot build character and courage by taking away men's initiative and independence. You cannot help men permanently by doing for them what they could and should do for themselves.*
>
> —William Boetcker, American religious leader and
> public speaker

★★★══ QUESTIONS TO PONDER

- How does the national debt affect your life and the lives of the next generations?

- How many types of taxes can you think of beyond income tax, sales tax, and real estate tax?

- Why do you think politicians spend money much more recklessly than most households and businesses?

12. Citizens Held Hostage to Political Power

We know that no one ever seizes power with the intention of relinquishing it.

—George Orwell, *1984*

There are many loud voices attempting to establish the new culture of America. One of the loudest is that of the career politician and their accomplices, who have had many decades to redefine the American culture in their own way, oftentimes disconnected from the realities understood by everyday Americans. I describe a career politician as someone who has been able to work the system to his or her advantage while giving the impression that he or she is helping others. We may not respect career politicians, but they have found many ways to obtain power and influence redefining the American way over the past several decades, and we are increasingly held hostage to their ever-expanding power.

Sometimes we use overly dramatic words to help make our points. For example, President Obama used the word hostage as a metaphor seventy times during his first four years as president to emphasize points related to taxes, immigration, jobs, the environment, health care, confirmations, and financial regulations.[13] This is a rather dramatic use of a very strong word, yet it helped to emphasize his points. Provocative words can catch our attention. With this in mind, I believe many American citizens are being held hostage to politicians and their political influence by redirecting the ways things should be in the nation. Theirs are unhealthy voices that push for further allegiance to more public programs to take care of more needs and a movement away from self-sufficiency. To further illustrate this point, I believe many in America are suffering from a sister mind-set to Stockholm syndrome.

Stockholm syndrome is defined as a condition that causes hostages to develop a psychological alliance with their captors as a survival strategy. These feelings result from bonds formed during time spent together and are generally considered irrational in light of the danger endured by the victims. These hostages look blindly at their captors as leaders and allow them to control their lives, even though they provide more harm than benefit. Doesn't that sound eerily similar to the way many view their politicians? When our energies are overly focused on whether any particular president will make our lives dramatically better or worse, we are allowing others to have more control of our lives than we should.

As a nation that prospered and grew with a focus on the power of individuals to make positive impacts on their communities, this is a sad state of affairs. Our personal powers have shrunk, and our public powers have overwhelmed and suffocated far too many of us. And with a monstrous beast in power, along with many accomplices looking to expand that power even more, untangling ourselves from this beast can be dangerous to our psyche because we have grown accustomed to giving away more of our rights to a sovereign state. The Constitution served us well to prevent this beast from growing for more than two hundred years, but our new government has found many ways to work around these restrictions to grow its influence beyond what is best for a healthy nation.

As the American spirit has become more enslaved to the excessive power of career politicians, we struggle to identify an escape plan or adapt to this dangerous condition. Many reluctantly adjust and live with this new normal while grumbling about their lost freedoms. Others strive to remove these shackles, but voting in a new political power who hears and respects the heartbeat of mainstream America is a challenge in many communities across America. The American who cherishes his or her ability to live independently often feels trapped and discouraged.

Exacerbating the political expansion against the heartbeat of America is the career politician. Even with low approval ratings in many cases, incumbents have become nearly unbeatable in many parts of our nation. With name recognition combined with money from lobbyists and other special interests acting as formidable deterrents to challengers, career incumbents are the new American way in our political arena. Here are some reasons why politicians almost always get reelected and continue to abuse their positions by expanding power and influence over their citizens:

- Name recognition is critical in elections, and it is already there for incumbents;

- Support is often available from other insiders and accomplices for expanding the system;

- Career politicians have a built-in understanding of what it takes to appease voters and win votes, even if it means saying things that are inconsistent with their voting records;

- They use public dollars to spin their voting records the way they believe you want; and

- Campaign materials are already in place to help keep reelection campaign costs down in comparison to those of new candidates.

Transitioning from the rhetoric of a Stockholm syndrome analogy, we simply have many American citizens today who worship the importance of government more than God and/or family. It is an unhealthy addiction to think government truly is going to help improve our lives. Though government assistance fails more often than not, far too many keep insisting that this is our best option, especially when we can use somebody else's money. It seems we may want to stop and ask if these social ills might have been caused by our rapid expansion of government programs that masquerade as short-term aid but fail in the end when they destroy human initiative. At some point, we may want to look at who has a more vested interest in solving our personal problems: our unknown politicians or God and family members who know us better and desire a stronger future for us?

As we look toward our nation's future, it can be disheartening to see the increasing belief that socialism is better than capitalism. This movement validates the concerns of freedom-loving Americans that the new American way includes an unhealthy dose of even more government dependence. We are reminded that the spirit of our youth is most energized when people take an interest in their well-being and inspire them to be the best people they can be. Politicians have become effective in showing our youth that they care: let's face it, they have to be to get elected. In just a few short decades, our politicians have accomplished their goal of increasing state-dependence of our innocent youth for more political power. These politicians may be persuasive in giving the impression they care, but their degree of influence in making us stronger long term is extremely limited because their answers almost always rely on greater dependence on government and not individual growth and personal responsibility. As a result, we lower our healthy skepticism and naively adjust to a new normal of overreliance on an impersonal politician to take care of our needs, and we become frustrated when this new mentor fails to help us reach our full potential.

Reaching our God-given potential requires sacrifice and hard work, which in the end make us stronger and are intrinsically more satisfying. Under the new American way, we have replaced President John F. Kennedy's admonition of "Ask what you can do for your country" with a new mind-set of "What free program can I get from my government?" As unhealthy expectations have expanded our nation from a place that provides us with liberty, freedom, and security to one that provides us with the mistitled benefits of free health care and free college (someone must be paying the doctors and teachers, right?), we have become spoiled and entrapped in a false state of mind that appeals to the new American psyche.

How crazy and out of control is our government, one that was established to focus on freedom and liberty with minimal interference from elected officials? The average American now pays taxes to anywhere from ten to twenty or more different governmental agencies and taxing authorities (federal taxes, state taxes, local taxes, school boards, regional commissions, housing authorities, environmental public authorities, etc.). Government power and control eat away at the American spirit as our identity radically switches from independence to government dependence. Let's review some of the taxes that are paid by many Americans:

Federal: Income tax, payroll tax, federal highway fees/tolls, capital gains tax, firearms and ammunition tax, brewers excise tax, tariffs;

State: Sales tax, income tax, state highway/gasoline tax, tobacco and alcohol tax; and

Local: Property tax, school board taxes and levies, stadium tax, watershed or lake district tax, regional development authorities taxes, economic development authorities taxes, hotel tax, city taxes, township taxes, county taxes, wheelage/road taxes, rental car tax, airport tax, etc.

We the people have lost personal ownership of our government as we increasingly recognize that politicians are in control, and regaining that control takes more energy than most are willing to give. This is a very sad commentary on America today. A significant percentage of Americans are fed up with the lies, the lack of honor in public service, and the power games that the political elites run with the high cost borne by the people watching their country collapse from within. Many concerned citizens feel hopeless that America is lost, and finding its way back home to a nation predicated on self-dependence over state dependence is difficult to visualize. We become enslaved by our captors, a Goliath government.

The cultural divide in America today has expanded into the political arena. While many debate right versus left in our political conversations, the real question is do we want citizens to become self-sufficient or state dependent? And if we desire freedom and self-sufficiency, how do we go about untangling ourselves from the long tentacles of a government that surrounds us from every direction before it's too late and there is no turning back?

> As long as enough people can be frightened, then all people can be ruled. That is how it works in a democratic system and mass fear becomes the ticket to destroy rights across the board.
> —James Bovard

★★★═══ QUESTIONS TO PONDER

- Why do you think most Americans are afraid to speak out against abuses undertaken by their government?

- What are some ways politicians work toward increasing their power over the people they are elected to serve?

- How do you think politicians trick us into believing their campaign promises?

- Do you know anyone who has an unhealthy belief that government is the best answer to fixing their problems? If so, why do you think they feel that way?

13. Undermining National Unity via Political Correctness

The jaws of power are always open to devour, and her arm is always stretched out, if possible, to destroy the freedom of thinking, speaking, and writing.
—John Adams, first vice president and second president of
the United States

Language means everything. It has the power to move us in many directions. The ability to communicate with creative, meaningful words is a healthy and productive way to connect us with others throughout the world. Open communication is fundamental to shaping our nation, and it is preserved in our treasured First Amendment. Conversely, public communications that deliberately revise the stories of the day or restrict the choice of words citizens are allowed to use limit our ability to communicate openly and honestly with our elected officials. A strong citizen-led government functions best when there is open, honest, two-way communication between citizens and their elected officials. Unfortunately, we have a severe shortage of honest dialogue going on between our government and its citizens on many levels.

Wouldn't you like to believe our elected officials would want unity and open communication with their citizens? That is, after all, what public service is all about, isn't it? This seems like a fair expectation; however, once we realize that political office is all about power and control, it becomes easier to understand why they do the things they do. If our politicians are able to gain control of the dialogue of our culture, it becomes easier for them to increase their power when stories are manufactured that cause citizens to divide and dilute their collective voice. This divisive approach has been undertaken by many of America's politicians in recent decades through the deliberate use of misinformation and the suppression of open speaking through political correctness (PC). Since politicians who are seen deliberately misinforming their electorate are unlikely to remain in power, they often utilize political accomplices to help misinform us in ways that undermine our national unity and increase their political power.

Political accomplices include many from our media, special interest groups, lobbyists, social networks, and many more. The primary goal of accomplices is to help the politicians increase their power. Political accomplices essentially serve as promoters of greater public dependence, and they are nicely rewarded by their political friends. These slanted stories are disconnected and often contrary to many of the real stories facing mainstream America.

How badly is political correctness constraining the American spirit? According to an August 24, 2017, poll by The Daily Wire, only 28 percent of conservative Americans believe they have true freedom of speech today, and most think the country is too politically correct.[14] This public pressure to conform to new societal norms is restricting our creative ability to think and communicate in a direct manner because we are coerced and at times even forced to constrain our voice behind political barriers. It invites the question, "Who is in charge of our language, the citizen or the government?" There is no question that most Americans cherish their freedom to speak, so why do so few believe they have true freedom of speech in our nation today? The reason only 28 percent of conservative Americans believe they have true freedom of speech is that, like many other foundational rights in the American way, this right is being reduced by increased government power and a corollary reduction in the power of the citizen. Conservative citizens in particular feel the pain of speech limitations inflicted on them by our government and some institutions of higher learning.

The most obvious political accomplices are media personnel and organizations who create fake or misleading stories to suit their specific agendas. After watching a television station literally cut and paste two completely different sentences together to drastically change a political story, it is not difficult to see that many in the media bring us the story they want to tell, instead of factually reporting the real news. Besides deliberately revising stories to fit an agenda, there are many in the media who speak with a strong bias that the public sector is the best solution to a myriad of problems. In many ways, our media sets the tone for the news of the day, and in many ways, their stories do not reflect mainstream American values of independence and self-responsibility.

After modifying the news of the day, politicians and their accomplices utilize PC measures to coerce citizens to embrace this new publicly acceptable language. PC can be defined as *controlling the language we use as determined by an authoritarian organization with the goal of minimizing conflict and expanding tolerance, especially among those identified as disadvantaged.* Another definition of PC is *conforming to a belief that language and practices which could offend political sensibilities (as in matters of sex or race) should be eliminated.* PC attempts to suppress the voice of the citizen through the threat of consequences for failure to follow this new public standard. Fear causes us to put up our guard and limits our freedom to think and express our ideas in a productive manner. When we allow this, we further expand our dependence on the politician and their accomplices to define new communication dos and don'ts, and our nation divides as we squabble over the simplest tasks, such as how we greet each other without offending anyone.

As part of the PC movement, we have softened the meaning of winners and losers by coddling failure. This softer approach goes against the American virtue of personal accountability in which we grow by overcoming challenges and build stronger character through individual dedication and persistence. Most stories of American greatness result from the tireless work of persistent individuals who overcome great adversity to accomplish great things. PC has weakened us as a nation as it detracts from our ability to communicate directly with those around us. It is polarizing and divisive; there are already consequences in place for not being respectful toward others that come out naturally through the marketplace and in our social relationships. Forced relationships using PC as the communications bridge are simply unnatural and unhealthy.

In a nation where citizens have been blessed with the ability to speak their minds, for better or worse, for much of our history, PC is dangerous. For example, one controversial PC movement that has circulated in some diversity programs at schools around the nation is restricting the use of the phrase and symbolism associated with "Merry Christmas" as it may be considered offensive to some.[15] Thankfully, most schools that have contemplated this type of movement received significant pushback before they were able to fully implement the idea, but the movement to consider such a policy is definitely alive in the mind-set of many diversity groups. In a nation that overwhelmingly defines itself as Christian, have we gone so far that we cannot even acknowledge a holiday that most of the world has celebrated for hundreds of years?

Even if someone does not embrace any given holiday, is it truly offensive for them to hear a greeting that may mean something to the person giving the salutation? How about those who hate mornings; should we restrict students from being able to say "Good morning" to others as we might offend someone who hates mornings? Are we now that thin-skinned that we cannot greet someone with words related to a holiday, a national holiday at that? Below are some examples of the hypocrisy of banning "Merry Christmas" salutations:

- Some want to limit our use of the term "Merry Christmas," yet they have no problem taking that day off work as a paid holiday;

- PC proclaims to promote diversity yet limits reference to one of the largest religions;

- Most PC efforts insert something like the following: "If you are unsure whether or not something is politically correct, come see us" (i.e., "We have the power to control what you say, not you"); and

- PC attempts to intimidate those who want to express their individual opinions.

More often than not, PC efforts backfire and stir up dissension and resentment in those who are not allowed to speak their minds. Most people resent being told what to think instead of being given the option of thinking for themselves about various issues. PC can be seen as an offensive dumbing down of America similar to the Stockholm syndrome, in which we are held captive to using only the language our captors allow us to use. PC is essentially a form of mind control. Striving toward the relatively pure goal of increasing tolerance in humankind, PC efforts too often result in the unintended consequence of increasing animosity, as Jacques Barzun, a French-American historian, states: "Political correctness does not legislate tolerance; it only organizes hatred."

The ultimate danger of PC is when it becomes public law or a policy requirement for the private sector. When we allow government the power to punish speech deemed harmful or offensive, especially when these laws are based largely on subjective opinions of whoever has power at the time, we set a dangerous precedent that exacerbates the potential for increased mind control and less freedom for the citizens of our nation. In a society where our respect for politicians is horribly low, especially as we assess the integrity and ability of our politicians to speak honestly with us, do we really want to empower them to define our language?

Human potential is unleashed when we are free to fully communicate with our hearts and our minds. America has accomplished much in the world economy with the full backing of the First Amendment to fine-tune the best choice of words we use to express the value of our products and services. Constraining these voices squashes the passion of citizens to speak their beliefs in ways they see fit. The ever-growing attempts by authoritarian groups to dictate what words we use is damaging and sets a scary precedent for our nation's future. Those hurt will include:

- Citizens, who are no longer able to freely speak critically about the issues of the day;

- Businesses, which are hamstrung in how they communicate production and value with employees and the marketplace; and

- Our nation, as we abandon the blessings afforded by our exceptional First Amendment.

  Here's a nation, one of the founding pillars was freedom of speech and freedom of expression. And yet, we have imposed upon people restrictions on what they can say, on what they can think. And the media is the largest proponent of this, crucifying people who say things really quite innocently.

—Ben Carson, politician, author, neurosurgeon, and current
secretary of Housing and Urban Development

★★★═══ QUESTIONS TO PONDER

- What are some of the most extreme examples of media bias you have observed?

- What attempts to insert politically correct terms have you found most offensive?

- How do you think political correctness efforts create division?

- What problems do you see resulting from political correctness going too far?

14. Replacing Public Order with Chaos

Civilization begins with order, grows with liberty, and dies with chaos.
—Will Durant, American writer, historian, and philosopher

Principles matter, especially for organizations like our government. Integrity matters, especially for those in leadership of our government. And when our lawmakers fail miserably in these two areas, public order is replaced with chaos. Unfortunately, this is the new America, one filled with chaos and incivility. But how did we get to this point, and why is it getting worse?

The job of a lawmaker is to establish laws that preserve public order. Once fair and just laws are established, they are enforced by professionals like police, firefighters, and the military to preserve public safety. Public laws are first established by our elected officials and then supported with public budgets. If an elected official can claim greater instability, they can justify the expansion of their base of operations to curtail these challenges. The primary reason America's public order has been replaced with chaos is that many politicians and their accomplices have inserted an illusion of instability to perpetuate their strong foothold on public opinion. This justifies their expanded influence to fix more problems that many times do not even exist or are greatly exaggerated.

America's first notable program to provide a safety net for its citizens was created in 1935 with Franklin Delano Roosevelt's Social Security program. As FDR stated in his support of this new program, it was created to serve as an insurance measure "against the hazards and vicissitudes of life." The intent of providing a government-sponsored safety net has some merit, while raising some concerns. The program would probably have been much better if politicians had set up the budget process and left it alone. But over the years, the opportunities for politicians to expand public programs with other people's money had just too strong an appeal for those addicted to OPM. The new American mind-set shifted from service and frugality to ways to help more and more of the less fortunate with other people's money, and political power began its growth to overtake a citizen-led government. Politicians ever since have operated with an ever-increasing addiction to OPM. Instead of stealing to support their OPM addiction, politicians use this approach to support this habit:

- They first create an illusion or exaggeration of a problem so they can justify an increase in their power and gain the backing of enough people to support fixing the problem;
- Their energies focus on expanding these entitlements while minimizing the pains associated with the providers of these funds; and

- Feeling empowered that our money is now theirs, politicians frequently redirect funds to other programs that help them get reelected and stay in power.

When politicians treat our money like it is theirs and they choose to spend it foolishly, citizen frustrations grow. When economic producers see their investment in the political system move away from public safety toward programs that expand political power and reward mediocrity, theft, and incompetence, citizens get frustrated. As we said earlier, it is very easy for politicians addicted to OPM to continue this practice until people say, "Enough is enough," and they resist. When they have fooled us into believing there are more public needs that government can take care of with other people's money, it becomes easier for us to let down our guard. We have been fooled into thinking they care about us when it is far too often themselves and their power that they really care about. And that money we thought was ours is now theirs.

How chaotic is America today? We certainly have our share of problems, but these social issues have been with us since our nation was founded. The only difference is, we are now exposed to the chaos on a never-ending basis with news media and social media covering virtually every protest. We are given the perception that things are more chaotic than they really are as media coverage focuses on the injustices around us, real or perceived, on a regular basis. When you add the bias of political accomplices who speak out against the traditional constitutional values that America was founded on, you have a loud voice going on throughout much of our nation that speaks for further change and power in the hands of government. These protests become frustrating to law-abiding citizens when they are allowed and sometimes even promoted by our lawmakers.

How do you feel when politicians blatantly disregard laws and ask us to pay for this new way? Join the list of frustrated citizens, as Americans everywhere are frustrated by the hypocrisy of our politicians who enact laws for us to follow, but not themselves. Unfortunately, far too many of our lawmakers have enacted laws that seem to follow this twisted form of logic:

- Law-abiding citizens are the first ones they tax to support illegitimate laws;

- Law-abiding citizens are the last ones they consider when enacting laws; and

- Law-abiding citizens are the first ones they punish when bad things happen.

Does the scenario above sound familiar? Isn't it sad when lawlessness is promoted at the expense of the taxpayer? The new America culture is riddled with chaos and incivility, and things appear to be getting worse. According to a KRC Research article from February 2, 2016, 70 percent of Americans consider our incivility to be at a crisis level.[16] The survey goes on to say that 58 percent of Americans expect incivility to get worse, and politicians, social media, and news media are identified as the three largest instigators of this new normal.

Another example of public lawlessness that is creating frustration and chaos for those who believe we are innocent until proven guilty is civil asset forfeiture. Civil asset forfeiture allows police to seize—and then keep or sell—any property they allege was involved in a crime. Owners need not ever be arrested or convicted of a crime for their cash, cars, or even real estate to be taken away permanently by the government. This initiative is now being undertaken by some communities as a money generator rather than a crime-stopping initiative, and this endeavor even inspired the television show *Miami Vice* in the 1980s.[17]

As I speak with military veterans around the nation, one of the more common questions I hear is: "Why does our government often prioritize public funds to assist citizens who have invested little in our nation over those who have served in defense of our nation?" Let's look at a couple of examples.

Hennepin County, Minnesota, recently set up a pilot program and funded it with $250,000 in tax dollars to help "illegal" immigrants find legal defense aid within their county.[18] So our elected officials are using $250,000 of our hard-earned tax dollars to help support those who are here illegally. This approach was never used earlier in our history when so many of our ancestors came here legally. Many of our ancestors had to meet important immigration requirements to ensure they had an interest in integrating the legal American way with our customs and constitutional law of the land. When one remembers that for the politician, personal power is more important than obeying the law, it becomes a bit easier to understand.

According to the Federation for American Immigration Reform (FAIR), our federal, state, and local governments spent approximately $135 billion per year for 12.5 million illegal adult immigrants, an average of $10,800 per year.[19] This is more than some of our senior citizens make in Social Security per year, something they funded themselves over many years. It is also not much different than what an enlisted National Guard or Army Reserves soldier makes per year in retirement after twenty years of service in defense of our nation. Is it fair for those who have contributed much to the betterment of our nation to reward others who have contributed less to our nation with similar compensation?

When the government places more economic value on "assisting" illegal immigrants who have previously invested little, if anything, in taxes, than on legal citizens who have invested much in the building of our nation, we have a major flaw in the system. Besides creating chaos and frustration, this also leads to a higher-entitlement and lawless society where people are paid to live here, and their law-breaking is forgiven. For those who jumped many hurdles to come to America legally in the past, this is totally unacceptable. Constitutional law does not even apply to sanctuary cities, where local government officials have decided that illegal immigrants are acceptable to our nation. This is a slap in the face to all legal immigrants.

Instilling consequences that are just and fair is critical to maintaining public order. Setting up public funds to assist illegal immigrants may appear to be nice, but it is not. In fact, it is disrespectful to those who chose to obey the law and pay their taxes for a process that supports enforcement of our laws rather than openly defying it. If we break the law, we know there are consequences if we are caught and prosecuted. If we let our family down during a time of need, we know there are consequences. When our businesses do something poorly, there are consequences. So why is it that there are very few consequences for our elected officials when they lie to us, cheat on us, or take actions that support illegal activities? We have a double standard in America, as politicians have set up a system in which they are far too often above the law and/or live by a different set of rules. The results of this hypocrisy include:

- Exempting themselves from following the law as they are now above the law;

- Defiantly opposing their oaths of office and the Constitution they swore to uphold;

- Allowing special interest groups that fit their political agenda to break the law; and

- Making it extremely difficult for our incredible law enforcers to do their jobs.

One of the first things I learned in the military was to respect others, especially those in authority. This can be a daunting challenge in a society in which we are encouraged to "speak our minds" about others in ways that may or may not improve a given situation. We just survived a divisive presidential election in 2016, in which most Americans seemed to despise one or both of the candidates, and what was lost was the respect for the position of president of the United States. Personalities can be divisive, but losing respect for the principles that guide a great nation can be detrimental to our future.

As we look at the civil unrest in our nation, it hurts. A relatively orderly nation has become chaotic. We see a nation that for many years fostered unity and patriotism and worked together to take on adversities. For those who remember the days following the 9/11 attack, it was uplifting to see Americans come together, united across many political, racial, socioeconomic, and other barriers, to say we wanted a safe nation and wanted to preserve the blessings we had. How quickly we forget to put aside our differences for the sake of our nation and instead argue over things that are relatively minor in comparison. When America loses its unity and focus on enforcing public order, chaos results, and we all suffer.

> *We focus so much on our differences, and that is creating, I think, a lot of chaos and negativity and bullying in the world.*
> —Ellen DeGeneres, American comedian and television host

★★★▬▬ QUESTIONS TO PONDER

- What ideas would you suggest for treating politicians' OPM addiction? Is a cure even possible?

- Why do you think some communities allow illegal protests to occur?

- How has chaos affected your life at home, work, or school?

15. A Future of Doom and Gloom

America will never be destroyed from the outside. If we falter and lose our freedoms, it will be because we destroyed ourselves.
—Abraham Lincoln, sixteenth president of the United States

Gallup polls show a growing percentage of Americans believe the next generation will be worse off than the current generation.[20] This is a very sad commentary on the social climate of our nation because America has historically been known as a place filled with optimism. Our nation's promise of opportunity and security for the next generation has been replaced with serious challenges and dangers.

If we look objectively at the facts, the great American experiment is in serious jeopardy of imploding from within. Part of the problem is the inability of many to identify acceptable solutions without a strong political or personal bias. America's world power and economic influence have been reduced, frustrating productive, hardworking Americans who are growing weary of financing problems created by politicians. America has very few elected officials who will support realistic budgets with reasonable constraints in a nation where the priority of security and economic sustainability has been replaced with a new focus on increasing political power and facilitating the expansion of our entitlement society.

Without a change for the better, we are dismantling a once-promising nation. As our nation fights over whether our future identity will be as a citizen-led or government-led nation, our frustrations increase, and a doom-and-gloom attitude expands due to:

- An increasing lack of trust in our public officials to solve even the simplest of problems;

- Divisiveness increasing over the changing cultural mind-set of governing the old way (citizen power) versus the new way (government power);

- Hardworking Americans growing weary of paying more in taxes than housing, food, and clothing as a whole in our nation;

- Concerned citizens losing hope when fighting against the Goliath that controls us from our nation's capital, where many now sadly refer to the District of Columbia as "Don't Care" or "the Swamp";

- A desire by many to erase our glorious history and create new storylines that undermine the traditional American values that helped make our nation strong; and

- An out-of-control debt and an expanded entitlement mentality that makes the future challenging for the next generation to reestablish a sound, realistic financial infrastructure.

As one concerned citizen once told me, "America has the best political system money can buy." In their never-ending pursuit of increasing their power, career politicians have been effective in expanding their control while citizens get left behind to pay for their mistakes. And when we consider that we pay politicians much more than we do our military service members, it may be time to reassess our priorities. As I discussed in my first book *Fixing America's Shattered Politics*, many politicians earn three or four times as much as our military for a similar level of responsibility, even though the obligations and sacrifices of our military are much greater.

America's politicians are surrounded by voices much louder than that of the average citizen, and we feel increasingly unable to influence the political process. Public services provided by our government were originally designed to directly serve the people, but this has been reversed as lobbyists, the media, and other stakeholders holding camp in the "public swamp" are there to protect their interests at the costs of others. This is a very serious issue, not only in our nation's capital, but also at many state and local levels of government. It becomes easier for these politicians and their accomplices to maintain power when their opposition, the citizen, puts up less resistance.

Americans who believe in limited government, welfare reform, and states' rights need to realize that a dangerous ideology is rapidly gaining momentum. In an interesting article that appeared in the *National Review* in 2017, David Nammo makes the comment that Americans hold social-ism in a higher regard than those in nations that have suffered under it.[21] Sometimes the grass may appear greener on the other side, but once you get there, it could end up being worse than the place you left. As several generations have been taught a lie about the benefits of expanded govern-ment, many have bought into this ideology without knowing its dangers. As we remove the truth of the incredible blessings, benefits, and privileges of American citizenship, the promise of a new way becomes easier to sell. But it is not a new way; it is a failed way, as many around the world unfor-tunately already know.

Before we move on to the opportunities concerned citizens have to restore hope across America, let's summarize the challenges discussed in this sec-tion of the book. America's greatest challenges include:

- Opponents of America's values are working hard to redefine the American way into a new and better way by creating division and confusion about the importance and relevance of our traditional citizen-focused values;

- The defining characteristic of our society breakdown is that Americans trust very few politicians or their accomplices;

- The average hardworking taxpayer does not make the list of top five friends of the average politician unless they are contributing to the politician's political power;

- America's foundation of limited government has changed to a significant amount of government;

- Many Americans look blindly at their politicians as their captors, allowing them to control their lives even though they provide more harm than benefit;

- Many politicians and their accomplices have been able to gain control of the dialogue of our culture, making it easier for them to increase their power when stories are manufactured, which causes citizens to divide and dilutes their collective voice; and

- America's public order has been replaced with chaos as many politicians and their accomplices have inserted an illusion of instability to perpetuate their strong foothold in public opinion.

America's greatest challenge today is the expanded belief of our citizens that more government will make their lives more fulfilling and our nation better. There simply is no historical proof that this works, but the appeal has been strong for many nations. America was founded on greatness, and we can return to greatness with a serious movement and return to a citizen-led government that prospers and protects the rights of the individual and makes our elected officials truly accountable to we the people.

> *Experience hath shewn, that even under the best forms of government those entrusted with power have, in time, and by slow operations, perverted it into tyranny.*
> —Thomas Jefferson, principal author of the Declaration of the Independence and third president of the United States

★★★═══ QUESTIONS TO PONDER

- What is the best hope for America's future?

- Why do you think a majority of Americans have lost hope for our future?

- How do you envision America returning to a genuine constitutional republic with a limited, respected government?

IV.

Opportunities

A pessimist sees the difficulty in every opportunity; an optimist sees the opportunity in every difficulty.

—Winston Churchill, former British Prime Minister, 1940-1945 and 1951-1955

Most people will sacrifice much for loved ones or causes that are intrinsically imbedded in their hearts. For most, this generally includes God; family; community or country; and other charitable, business, or school programs in their area. Our nation thrived as a unique place where the opportunity to pursue our dreams was made possible for many when our focus was God, family, and country. However, this great nation is facing an identity crisis and needs help to reclaim our first love: individual independence. This fight to regain our nation's first love will require men and women to stand up for what is right. Our journey to regain America's foundational principles will be rocky; politicians and their accomplices love their grip on the power and dollars that go with it. However, for the future of our nation and for the sake of our children, we owe it to them to take a stand about where this nation is headed, don't we? When we see danger, let's find a different road to take, and let's do it before we fall off the cliff. Our nation is going in the opposite direction from its original intent, but we have the power, through active civic engagement and a sense of urgency, to bring it back.

So how do we reverse our nation's course?

We know there are enemies of freedom in self-serving politicians and their accomplices who want even more power and control at a very high cost to we the people. Their addiction to OPM is destroying our financial security and is removing our traditional value of individual independence. Americans are tired of the lies and deceit of our elected officials and their empty political promises. When we assess their unacceptable actions, it can be frustrating. If we could only harness, say, 10 to 20 percent of that legitimate negative energy into positive action, we could restore America as one nation under God, with liberty and justice for all, before it is too late. America, the land of the free because of the brave, needs the help of concerned citizens to bring back public accountability, one community at a time across the country. While many complain about our politicians, we must go on as a society. The important questions each of us must reflect on are:

How do we go forward as a society, and what is my role in shaping a stronger future, one that preserves freedom, liberty, and justice for all?

Regardless of who we support for president or what political party we believe best represents our interests, America is rapidly evolving before our eyes, and civic input is critical to shaping this future. It is time to move past our oftentimes relatively minor differences and focus on the tasks that bring us together, as we did after 9/11. We work better when we learn from our past and focus on identifying positive steps we can take to make our nation stronger now and for future generations.

As we look back at the challenges facing our nation in Part III, the primary one is a persistent movement from some to redefine the American way in a manner that transitions our focus from individual-independence to government-dependence. The allure of someone else paying for our wants has overtaken many in our society. I pointed out that this is a dangerous precedent because this Utopian perspective may sound nice but does not work in social contracts. America will be stronger going forward if we can move back to a cultural mind-set in which we understand that self-sufficiency benefits all of us. Most parents know this and raise their children to grow into self-reliant independent young adults. The alarming thing is that many political officials want the government to become our primary caretaking option, even as many struggle to manage their own affairs. We have an opportunity to change the cultural mind-set of America back to a rugged, independent, self-sufficient one that makes each of us stronger. America's system of limited government empowers citizens to achieve a higher level of self-actualization to reach their God-given potential better than any bureaucratic, impersonal public program.

Another one of the bigger challenges facing America is that many do not see the degree of the crisis before us because they have grown accustomed to the government controlling more and more of our lives. They do not see imminent danger. But let's not be mistaken: the deliberate effort to overhaul the heart and soul of our nation's identity is dividing us, and by the time it becomes defined as a genuine problem by enough citizens, it may be too late. The sooner we recognize the shenanigans our elected officials play on citizens, the sooner we can do our part to help minimize these reckless actions. We need to employ a sense of urgency for Americans to take back our country from our out-of-control politicians. As Thomas Paine, author of *Common Sense*, said, "It is the duty of the patriot to protect his country from its government. We do this through accountability."

In today's challenging political climate, it can be very easy to be discouraged, to say this mess is too big for me to make an impact, but that attitude allows the problem to keep growing. Remember that when you make no decision, you truly are deciding on the status quo, and concerned citizens can no longer afford to stand idly by while the political elites and their accomplices bring this great nation down from within. Public accountability will be the key to improving our government, and civic engagement is the tool that will bring this together. Those who want to redefine America know that. Patriotic Americans who want to see our country return to its foundational values of independence and limited government will need to respond strongly because the voice of constraint is absent in far too many political jurisdictions. Civic engagement brings out the best of us, and our public officials need to hear the voice of passionate reason. Bridging the large gap between public trust and citizens begins when we demand honest, respectful answers from our elected officials. Rebuilding an honest dialogue with our elected officials can provide us with an opportunity to address the ever-growing need for public constraints and a reduction in the political addiction to OPM.

One definition of insanity is doing the same thing over and over and expecting different results. The out-of-control zest for power of our politicians will continue to exceed the American comfort zone without a strong, concerted effort by the citizens to regain control of their government. Saying no is very difficult in today's world of affluence and greed, but we must recognize the value in saying it to continued expenditures beyond our means (e.g., a $21-plus-trillion national debt).

In a constitutional government, each individual has a responsibility to be involved in *their* government. This responsibility requires a basic understanding of the nuances of government, including its roles and limitations, so that political pressure is focused in a manner that better serves our nation as a whole, not just specific groups. There is always a balancing act to consider; when one group receives some form of benefit, another group pays for it, a concept far too often neglected when public policy on entitlements is enacted. But a civic voice of persuasive reason can counter these imbalances.

Many Americans invest energy in bettering their family, work, school, and house of worship. When we balance these priorities within our limits of time and resources, we are typically contributing mightily to a greater community. This is the first step toward becoming a great American: taking care of business on our home front, however we decide to define that. The heartbeat of America starts in the household and moves out from there. The family is where most people invest most of their energy, concern, time, and talent. Worshipping God and the miracles that surround us is truly a blessing we can and should enjoy in a free nation. Protecting our nation from harm, both inside and outside its boundaries, is also critical to our safety and sustainability.

As a nation founded on individual responsibility, it is important to define those terms and what they look like in the public domain. From my perspective, I believe we are stronger individuals when we start with a belief that no one owes us anything, do our best to help others, and appreciate the blessings that come our way, including the process (hard work) that goes into receiving those blessings. As you reflect on your own definition, we all will have a stronger framework for assessing a critical question when it comes to choosing the candidate who earns our trust and vote:

> *Is the candidate and/or public official working for me and the future of my community, or are they working primarily for themselves and their own gains?*

This is also a great time in American history to ask what we stand for. It's a question that will be put to the test as the American culture and traditions are challenged in the days ahead. The pressure to be quiet has harmed many societies, and that form of pressure is certainly invading America in many ugly ways that go against our traditional values of respecting and even embracing civil discourse with respect for the nation in which we live.

It is time to ask ourselves whether we have had enough of the political and cultural challenges facing our nation and what efforts we can we realistically take to help right the ship within our own sphere of influence. We all can make a tremendous difference in shaping a better America. In the following chapters, let's explore some of the ways we can begin this journey toward making that happen.

> *A Republic, if you can keep it.*

> —Benjamin Franklin, September 7, 1787, in response to the question of whether America was a republic or a monarchy

★★★══ QUESTIONS TO PONDER

- What are some opportunities you believe may be possible for you to have a positive influence on America within your network of relationships?

- What lessons have you learned that you believe could be helpful in shaping a stronger America?

- What works to keep you accountable to your leaders?

- What parts of the political arena are you most interested in shaping for the better? Your local, state, or federal government or other political jurisdictions such as school boards?

16. It All Starts with Civic Leadership

Never doubt that a small group of thoughtful, committed citizens can change the world; indeed, it's the only thing that ever has.
—Margaret Mead, American cultural anthropologist

Whether you were born here or are a naturalized citizen, you have inherited a very special gift: American citizenship. And like many special gifts, it takes effort and perhaps even some sweat equity to fully appreciate its value. Parents experience the gift of the birth of children, as well as the work that goes into raising them into responsible adults. Marriage can be a special gift, but it takes sacrifice and love to keep it strong. Loving God can provide us with peace and purpose, but striving to honor God with our words and actions takes effort. We have an obligation to preserve the gift of our citizenship, perhaps even nurse it back to health. We can do this not just by voting every two or four years but by faithfully serving as patriotic citizens on a daily basis, doing our part to keep the American dream alive for future generations. Civic leadership is not a job or a career for most of us, but it is an opportunity to make an impact on our local communities and on our country. The future of our nation depends on civic leadership now more than ever.

Just as investing our energies into our family, faith, and profession is beneficial to our well-being, investing in civic engagement also has many rewards. Only a very small percentage of the people in the world have the privilege of living in a civic-led nation, where they have the opportunity to be the primary voice of public affairs. With this privilege comes responsibility, as well as great rewards. Civic engagement provides one of the better returns on investment we can receive as human beings as we influence our community for the better. It may not involve direct payment, but the rewards can be much greater as we serve a cause much bigger than ourselves. These rewards often include:

- Opportunity to truly shape the public opinion of our communities;

- Opportunity to keep elected officials accountable to their constituents;

- Opportunity to shape a public mission that aligns with your values;

- Opportunity to validate public opinion on key issues, such as protecting the First Amendment, which is valued by 85 percent of Americans versus 15 percent who prefer incorporation of political correctness; for PC;

- Opportunity to help elected officials identify ways to minimize tax burdens by speaking on behalf of reasonable constraints, limits, and boundaries;

- Opportunity to see firsthand which elected officials are serving their constituents, as well as which ones are not; and

- Other opportunities you believe are important for making your community stronger.

Civic involvement is a great investment in your future, similar to investing in a house. A house in itself is not an asset or a liability; it has a foundation, but it is always a work in progress. We the people "own" special houses in Washington, DC, (i.e., the White House and the US Capitol). If we invest in them, they will become assets; if we neglect them, they will become liabilities. Restoring the houses will require an investment by we the people to keep our elected officials accountable for stabilizing and even enhancing our special houses. Citizen accountability in improving our houses results in a win-win opportunity for America to move forward as a more united nation.

America was designed to be led by we the people. However, we have lost this power to politicians through years of letting our guard down. Regaining our rightful position as a truly civic-led nation will require dedication, persistence, and courage by many to stand up against those who have overtaken our nation and who use numerous bullying tactics to maintain their power. But truth is powerful, and motivated citizens have undertaken many amazing movements throughout our history. We can regain our country's status as a civic-led nation through dedicated civic leadership that inspires us to be all we can be as everyday citizens who strive to bring decency and honorable principles back into prominence within our country.

We cannot afford to have the American dream be taken away by naysayers who believe there is a better way than the one that has worked so effectively for more than two hundred years. As I speak around the country, it is always interesting to get answers from the audience to this basic question:

What does it mean to be a great American?

We can learn a lot about people and how their backgrounds influence their answers. As diverse as America is, the perfect answer can be difficult to determine, but the best answers typically start with an accurate and thorough understanding of the basics of the subject matter. A critical prerequisite for being a great American is understanding the law of the land, our Constitution, as well as other key documents that define our great nation. Another key aspect is to listen to how they view the importance of personal responsibility and independence. Answers to this question allow us to better understand how others see the world, including their own place within their community and their desire to serve a cause bigger than themselves, such as their God, family, or nation. I thoroughly enjoy speaking with our military and veterans because their answers almost always revolve around their passion for protecting the goodness of America's traditional values. For example, many veterans share the power of strong bonds they form with other service members as they undertake their jobs with a focus on teamwork, unity, and getting the job done rather than arguing over their petty differences.

Becoming a great American involves leadership that truly serves others first and embraces the goodness that results from personal responsibility and accountability. I believe America can be stronger if we incorporate more of the lessons learned from our service members into the political arena. My experience working with disabled veterans is that they are among the citizens most frustrated about our corrupt, broken political systems, and their insights into improving things are often profound. Many of these American heroes have felt the pain of bureaucratic responses to their needs for assistance in the healing of their emotional and physical scars as they readjust to life after stressful combat service. These are also some of the strongest Americans, and their voices should be heard in communities throughout America. They represent a great resource for fostering lessons that embrace honorable public service and have the power to bridge gaps between the military and civilians. The Minnesota Humanities Center and College of the Ozarks both do an excellent job of bringing many powerful military stories to life as helpful, applicable tools for improving communities throughout Minnesota and Missouri, for example.

Another example of a civic leader I've found to be inspiring and who stands strongly behind his political convictions is Mike Lindell, inventor and CEO of MyPillow. Mike's is a great Minnesota story of someone who overcame a crack cocaine habit, pursued his dream of inventing the most comfortable pillow on the market, and shares that story around the world. As he has become involved in various political conversations, Mike and his company have come under attack by some opposed to traditional American values. Mike has stood strong in his conviction that the traditional American way is to be cherished, supported, and promoted, even against strong opposition that threatens him and his company. His strong stand has earned further respect from many Americans who share his view that America is a great country in need of strong leadership.

America's lack of trust in our elected officials is considered by many to be one of the greatest challenges facing the country today. But strong civic leadership can be instrumental in closing this significant trust gap in a manner that benefits all. For people to have confidence and regain trust where it has been lost, we need to get back to the basics of communication so challenges and necessary solutions can be discussed with respect, integrity, and honesty between all parties. In G. Edward DeSeve's 2011 article "Regaining the Public's Trust," he discusses the six fundamentals needed to regain public trust. These are great principles to live by and demand in our elected officials:

- **Honesty:** The hallmark of earning anyone's trust. We must hold others accountable, letting them know we will not tolerate even small lies or a little bit of cheating. All strong organizations are based on a high level of ethics and accountability for one's actions, and civic leadership that enhances this part of our political communication facilitates tremendous steps toward bridging the lost trust between frustrated citizens and their elected officials.

- **Efficiency:** Making sure government delivers value for our hard-earned money. This includes incorporating productive private-sector practices and measuring efficiency with those limited resources so the public better understands what they are receiving for their taxes.

- **Transparency:** Perception is reality, and debating public policy in front of constituents provides genuine dialogue with interested stakeholders. Unfortunately, an overwhelming majority of public decisions are made in private. Civic engagement must demand that legitimate public policy decisions be made in public.

- **Accountability:** Telling people what you are going to do and then giving them an accounting of how it was done.

- **Good policy choices:** Starting with a baseline of understanding and differentiating between public needs and wants, civic leaders can oversee policy choices.

- **Positive outcomes:** Policy choices that are made honestly, efficiently, and with transparency and accountability are more likely to produce positive outcomes.[22]

Before we move on, I'm sure some of you may feel overwhelmed and unsure just how you can become an effective civic-minded leader. These doubts are real, but they can be overcome by good-hearted people who are committed to doing the right thing for their community. Below are some of the excuses I have heard from citizens on why they feel they are unable to contribute to the process before them, as well as some things you may want to consider when facing these doubts:

- **"I have no time."** Challenging for all of us, but it is critical that we find time, beginning with simple baby steps that are not so overwhelming. New habits take several weeks to formulate.

- **"I am unsure where or how to start."** Start with reading meeting minutes or attending public meetings.

- **"I am not familiar with how government works."** This can actually be a benefit to becoming a strong civic leader because you can begin without an agenda, and you have a more genuine desire to identify how your elected officials are honorably providing a public service to you. You deserve answers that make sense to you because it is your government.

- **"My voice will not make a difference."** The American political system is designed for everyday citizens to be active leaders in the course of its future, and the time for providing that input is now for a nation desperately in need of more civic leadership.

- **"I am fearful about speaking out against the status quo."** There are many who do not like the status quo in politics today, and those who speak for decency and positive change are highly respected by most Americans.

- **"I do not have the tools needed to make change."** We have some incredible tools available with technology that arguably should facilitate greater communication between elected officials and constituents. The needs for civic engagement vary tremendously, so utilize the tools you already have.

The following are several ways concerned citizens can be civically engaged in their communities at the local, state, and federal political levels:

- Be a vocal proponent for accountable public discourse by emailing or calling your elected officials and writing letters to the editor;

- Support efforts that go against the status quo if you are unhappy with politics as is;

- Think outside the box and ask elected officials challenging questions;

- Find and support alternative candidates who you believe best represent honor and integrity; and

- Participate in other activities that best fit your unique skills, passions, and abilities to make a positive difference in your community.

Civic duty is an important part of being an American. Your country believes in you and has entrusted you with the incredible opportunity to preserve it. Let's each identify how our interests and abilities can be best utilized to positively affect the civic process by putting these passions to work to shape a stronger America, both now and for future generations. Civic oversight of our government is the most powerful tool and best hope we have for bringing America back to a place of respect and service to we the people.

> *If there is one thing I've learned in my years on this planet, it's that the happiest and most fulfilled people I've known are those who devoted themselves to something bigger and more profound than merely their own self-interest.*
>
> —John Glenn (D), astronaut and US senator from Ohio

★★★═══ QUESTIONS TO PONDER

- What are some of your passions, and how can they be incorporated into civic duties?

- Why do you think many Americans expend little energy on civics?

- What role do you think honor and integrity play in teaching our children about strong civic engagement and political leadership?

17. Bringing Morals Back into Our Culture

Our Constitution was made only for a moral and religious people. It is wholly inadequate to the government of any other.

—John Adams

Politics are a reflection of our culture, and our culture has changed significantly in recent years. Values such as faith, family, and country have shifted toward more of an entitlement society, where government can be manipulated by citizens to meet more of our needs, as well as more of our wants. Due to this change over the past two generations, many millennials believe that socialism is better than our form of government. Socialism has failed numerous times in world history, but there are many who still think it will work. Socialism and other forms of large government will not work, especially in a nation that has strong roots in the values of freedom, liberty, and individual responsibility. Which way will America turn in the days ahead as citizens identify their preference for living in a nation of independence or government dependence? This question will be answered by the degree to which citizens return the positive effects of morality in our culture.

With a return to a culture of moral clarity, which defines boundaries and delineates acceptable public behavior, America's future has hope. Without it, chaos will increase, and anarchy will cause us to divide and eventually collapse from within. If our society continues to tolerate immoral or illegal activities, the government will end up replacing individual beliefs and charitable organizations in defining our new moral standards. For example, freedom for individuals to contribute to their favorite charities will no longer be financially incentivized as a tax deduction, and the government will gain further control through expanded confiscation of more of our personal finances. Short-term civic engagement is critical for slowing down the erosion of America; bringing morals back into our culture is our best hope for restoring America to its original purpose.

Morality has a negative connotation in today's PC world, but having a strong moral compass is truly one of the most important attributes for strong leadership. Morals guide us to do the right thing, even when no one is watching. Morality is critical in treating others fairly and not providing preferential treatment or inclusivity for certain groups. True morality is based on absolute truths about what is right and what is wrong, and they do not change to reflect new PC definitions. In fact, morality is generally the opposite of PC. Genuine morals emphasize fairness and genuine compassion for others, not forcing the special treatment of others via bullying or coercion.

In order to effectively bring morals into civic engagement, we need to recognize the importance of morals and how they directly shape the public sector. This can be challenging when morals are seen as taboo by some who believe they do not belong in the public domain. There could be nothing further from the truth; public law is based on the application of morality and justice to create civil order. To make an impact, we will need to effectively identify how moral values provide public value and civil order for our communities. This public dialogue can be challenging to have in today's PC world, but we must have these conversations to reverse the erosion of our cultural values before it's too late. We must be relentless in remembering that moral standards are beneficial for a civil society as they:

- Help establish fair and just laws that preserve strong public order;

- Validate the importance of individuals freely giving to charitable and faith-based activities they personally identify as best fixing societal problems;

- Provide a stronger emphasis on fairness for all stakeholders;

- Make it more feasible to live within our means, including paying down our debt (both personal and public); and

- Realign with our nation's core foundation of independence and restore hope for our future.

As we strive to bring an appreciation of the value of moral law back into America, we must look back to see when our culture changed and how it affects our society. We must consider its impact as well as its causes. Each person will answer these questions differently, depending on their individual perspectives. In his article "Why the Kids Are Socialists[23]," Devin C. Foley explains five primary reasons for an erosion of our cultural values:

- Broken homes: Divorce and broken families have gone from a small segment of our population to the new normal, and the struggles that go with these broken homes bring in new challenges;

- Education: The teaching of civics and American history has been replaced in many schools with political correctness and socialist-friendly ideologies;

- Christianity (religion): Faith used to be a guiding force for serving others but has been replaced by many citizens now wanting to be served by their government;

- Capitalism: This has been identified as a risky way of doing business and something that should be removed in favor of a larger government-security society; and

- Decadence: We have transitioned from purchasing necessities to taking on debt to pay for more wants; we have become an instant-demand society.

Laws based on a moral code have been created under every form of government in world history; the only question is which moral standards are to be utilized in shaping our public laws. American laws provide grace to allow immoral actions to occur because we are all sinners, but we must not intentionally reward immoral behavior as we have begun to do so in many areas. Even though some may find standards of morality to be offensive at first, in the end, I have found that most agree they are necessary for the orderly function of a civil society. Morals have the power to turn the heart around, especially when presented in a genuine, caring way. The power of living by a set of morals starts in the home. From there it evolves into our communities and, eventually, throughout our nation.

We are in the midst of a fight for the cultural soul of our nation, and we must stand strong for the values that built America into an exceptional nation. When I speak with high school and college audiences on the importance of morals in the public sector, a common response I hear is, "We do not want any morals imposed on the way we live." My response is typically something like this:

Morals have been a major factor in forming America's laws for more than two hundred years and most Americans want to live where just and fair laws preserve a healthy, respected, safe community for all. Moral law benefits all of us in a civilized nation. Laws based on moral clarity are the closest way they can be established in a fair manner. Any society operating without morals leads to chaos, dysfunction, and eventually anarchy.

Another question I often hear is, "Isn't it compassionate to have our government take care of those in need?" Caring about others is obviously a great humanitarian interest, but we must ask if it is genuine caring when we demand that someone else pay for our wishes so that we can feel good about ourselves. This is not compassion; it is, frankly, selfish. We show caring by personally investing ourselves, including our time, resources, and support of organizations and charities that we believe in, not needs we think others should be forced to pay for because they make us feel good. Fixing the problems of our society has been undertaken with great results by numerous charitable organizations throughout our country, whereas government attempts to fix problems have not.

Morals are not just about religion and rights and wrongs. They are also about living life in a productive, responsible, disciplined manner. They are about walking the talk, with accountability to others. Discipline is often one of the keys to achieving a higher level of moral conduct. Employers, schools, and our military are keenly aware of the importance of discipline as it strengthens their organizations by increasing accountability and productivity. Yet this is one attribute that is missing from many in today's culture. Responsible discipline starts with the individual, then evolves into the culture, then eventually becomes intertwined with political affairs. Discipline leads to productivity and value in many ways and should be supported by a healthy society.

Another important way to bring moral decency back into our national arena is by utilizing humor to make points of moral validity. Respectful humor can help soften tensions when discussing political differences with others. As comedian Mel Brooks says, "We seem to have lost the ability to be mutually self-deprecating as a result of our silly PC culture."[24] He goes on to say that sensitivity to the feelings of others is a good thing; however, he suggests that obliterating humor due to oversensitivity is unhealthy and that we are in trouble if we cannot laugh at ourselves and appreciate our differences. Sharing our passions and concerns with a sense of humor is more genuine and beneficial for the well-being of a healthy nation as well as individuals. Isn't that what we want in a nation that values free speech: to be able to speak with humor and passion about what is on our minds? Making our points with a respectful sense of humor can be great medicine, as well as an effective technique.

Personal courage is also critical to maintaining moral values. During my twenty-three years of military service, personal courage was critical in helping me make it through many challenges I had not seen before. Though those challenges were daunting at times, I came to the conclusion after six years in local politics that standing up to corruption also requires intense personal courage. The military offers a system that defends leaders when they do what is honorable and right, whereas in politics, right or wrong is less important than who has more clout. For example, when I caught one of our elected officials stealing $540, I was censured by the county board even though I was legally and morally right and the elected official admitted guilt by repaying the stolen funds. In the military, punishment would go to the person stealing, not the person catching the thief.

America needs more civic leadership to watch over a group that has earned a reputation as corrupt and devious in its ways of public service. Citizens must leverage their influence to request adoption of a code of ethics that guides elected officials in how they conduct public business. The Constitution and open meeting laws are incredible and powerful tools for managing the people's business; however, they are far too often disregarded by politicians who work around these laws to serve their own agenda. Public accountability initiated by citizens backed with a stated code of ethics or other measures is critical for improving the horrible situation we have, in which an overwhelming majority of public decisions are made in private.

Follow-through and accountability are critical for any efforts to succeed, especially in the political arena, where politicians have become skilled at skimming incoming funds for alternative purposes. For example, elected officials have determined that cigarettes are dangerous to our health, so they place higher penalty taxes on this product to help fix the problem. The problem is that these taxes are more often than not used for other purposes, and the original intent of fixing the identified problem is washed away. Higher revenue is generated, which politicians refuse to give back, and their original focus on using these funds to fix the problem disappears. This is all too common and explains the frustrations Americans feel about a poor or misappropriated use of their tax dollars.

Few public actions frustrate citizens more than observing elected officials blatantly making decisions that benefit themselves with little respect for acceptable boundaries. We need a government of stronger leaders who are going to say, "No more" to the ever-growing list of demands from various groups. Saying no to public demands can be difficult and unpopular, but many will agree it is the right way to stop the bleeding of our nation. Politicians simply have too much power to spend more resources on items that benefit their power, but not the people. Service over power guided by realistic, honest compassion is desperately needed throughout America's public arena today. This is taking the moral high road of living within our means publicly and restoring the importance of personal responsibility with the citizens of our communities. Some examples of how you can make a positive impact in your community include:

- Discuss the importance of genuine fairness for all stakeholders in the context of policy-making to help overcome political payoffs and/or biases;

- Ask for clarification on any real or even perceived conflicts of interest by public bodies; and

- Strive to find common bonds with other community stakeholders rather than focusing on differences, which can derail productive conversations.

Finally, moral clarity helps preserve safety, both for individuals and for a nation. Virtually every house has some form of security in place to protect loved ones. Allowing people to come into America illegally is not tolerance; it is breaking the law that is designed to protect us. Definitions mean everything. Illegal residents should not be given the same or, in many cases, higher levels of protection than legal residents. Most families do not allow strangers into their homes, and Americans are safest when we live by these same rules. For example, America's immigration policy used to be based on enforcing a legal process that defines the rights and obligations of citizens to enter our nation legally. When we strip away these definitions and allow anyone to enter our nation, legal or not, we give preferential treatment to illegal immigrants as compared to those who entered our nation legally. By taking the moral high road, we are not saying, "Do not come here," to future citizens wanting to come to America; we are saying, "Come here the legal way," like the rest of us.

Who is going to set America's moral compass going forward, we the people or our politicians? Standing up for decency in the political arena is critical today, as the dangers of our political actions are damaging our safety and security. America needs a revival in our culture of self-responsibility and respect for the great heritage of our nation for it to succeed into the foreseeable future. Investing in ways to bring moral clarity back into our culture will be one of the greatest opportunities we have as a society for Restoring Hope Across America!

> *In the first place, we should insist that if the immigrant who comes here in good faith becomes an American and assimilates himself to us, he shall be treated on an exact equality with*

everyone else, for it is an outrage to discriminate against any such man because of creed, or birthplace, or origin. But this is predicated upon the person's becoming in every facet an American and nothing but an American...There can be no divided allegiance here. Any man who says he is an American, but something else also, isn't an American at all. We have room but for one flag, the American flag...We have room for but one language here, and that is the English language...And we have room but for one sole loyalty and that is a loyalty to the American people.

—President Theodore Roosevelt

★★★═══ QUESTIONS TO PONDER

- Why do you think some politicians are able to get away with more selfish or immoral actions than those in most other professions?

- What moral values do you think are most important for America's future?

- Why do you think some Americans are opposed to the use of morals to help guide public order?

- How do you bring your moral perspectives into political discussions?

18. Pushing Back on Political Gluttony

Most of the things we buy are wants. And we call them needs, but they're wants.

—Dave Ramsey, American businessman, author and

radio host

Once citizens become engaged in civics with a moral compass, we can begin to push back on the gluttony that has overtaken our public sector. We must keep in perspective that the public sector has grown from essentially 10 percent of America's GDP to 40 percent in just a few generations, and there appears to be minimal slowdown in sight. In order to help concerned citizens push back, we will need budget information, identification of public priorities from our elected officials (hard to get from most public organizations), and then a strong familiarity with the Constitution and associated laws that protect citizens from political abuse. The average American pays about 40 percent of their income to about seventeen different taxing authorities, so the problem of political gluttony is very wide and very deep. (This figure is an average rate based on almost 30 percent base for various income taxes, social security taxes, and Medicare taxes plus an additional 10 percent for consumption-based taxes such as sales tax, property tax, or other taxes.) [25] Many people do not realize how many types of taxes they pay until they take a moment to look more closely at their bills as many of these taxes are somewhat hidden from view (for example, property taxes are often built into our house payments, so we may not know how high that tax is unless we look for it).

One of the strongest examples of pushing back on the dangers of political gluttony can be found in the story of Congressman Davy Crockett, often referred to as "Not Yours to Give[26]": The story of Davy Crockett and how Congress, and government in general, has no right or authority to give to charity. When considering a bill to appropriate tax dollars for the widow of a distinguished naval officer, Davy Crocket made the following argument to Congress on April 2, 1868:

> I have as much respect for the memory of the deceased and as much sympathy for the suffering of the living as any man in this house, but we must not permit our respect for the dead or our sympathy for a part of the living to lead us into an act of injustice to the balance of the living. I will not go into an argument to prove that Congress has no power to appropriate this money as an act of charity. Every member upon this floor knows it. We have the right, as individuals, to give as much of our own money as we please in charity; but as members of Congress we have no right so to appropriate a dollar of the public money.

> Every man in this House knows it is not a debt. We cannot, without the grossest corruption, appropriate this money as the payment of a debt. We have not the semblance of authority to appropriate it as a charity. I have said we have the right to give as much money of our own as we please. I am the poorest man on this floor. I cannot vote for this bill, but I will give one week's pay to the object, and if every member of Congress will do the same, it will amount to more than the bill asks.

How sad that a statement made 150 years ago rings even more true today as politicians recklessly abuse the limited financial resources of hardworking Americans. Wouldn't it be nice if politicians respected our hard-earned money in a manner in which fairness, respect, and national safety were more important than their addiction to OPM? Though the rationale to support a grieving widow who lost her husband in defense of our nation is an extremely powerful and righteous request in many ways, Congressman Crockett got it right in claiming that this was the appropriate place for charity, not government. The fact that not one member of Congress took up his offer to provide one week's salary to the grieving widow reveals much about how spending OPM is easier than spending one's own money for worthy causes.

Fast-forward 150 years and the American government now spends recklessly on so many crazy programs that provide minimal if any public value. The challenging part is that almost everyone knows this, yet eliminating or even reducing ineffective or obsolete government programs is virtually impossible without significant public outcry. Even the most useless government programs are passionately supported by politicians and their accomplices, even though those expenditures cost our nation public safety and prosperity in so many ways. Identifying these inefficiencies is rather easy to do when public budgets are available for concerned citizens to review. The challenging part is finding honorable men and women who will run for office and have the personal courage and conviction to treat OPM as if it were truly their own. We truly have no choice but to slow down this unsustainable growth, now.

Slowing down the unsustainable growth will help regain the trust and credibility between the public and private sectors. True leadership understands the root of a problem, and true leaders have the fortitude to take the steps necessary to resolve the problem by making tough decisions based on sound principles. Living within our means is a very sound principle. But finding officials to elect who will courageously take responsibility for turning around the nation's sinking ship may be difficult, though this is the most feasible solution for solving our nation's love affair with irresponsible spending.

This is a point I make with every audience I speak with:

Ensure your elected officials know and implement this: Givers have to set limits because takers do not have any.

Encouraging our elected officials at every level to respect the limited resources of taxpayers will result in some elected officials being pushed out by those in the political elite who are addicted to OPM. America needs more elected officials who are interested in honorably serving for the betterment of our country's future instead of their own agenda. Political service that is oriented toward the giver of tax funds rather than the receiver will require the support of concerned citizens who will help them overcome the resistance that comes with fighting the status quo of government gluttony and the corrupt system that has overtaken America in far too many political arenas. I have had numerous elected officials tell me their biggest challenge is that the average citizen believes their public budgets are essentially unlimited. Let's change that mind-set.

The sustainability of America begins with living within our means, something our government has failed miserably to do these past several years. In addition, a sustainable future will involve a much clearer focus from our citizens on what is important and what is not because we must prioritize and learn to say no to many luxuries we have become accustomed to enjoying. (Just as this is true for most families living check to check, it is also true with public budgets.) This is easier said than done, but we truly do not have any other choice as a nation. Our citizens must regain our lost government and demand transparency and accountability in the management of our nation.

The Constitution is essentially about boundaries and moral clarity. It provides boundaries on how public business is to be conducted in a way that fosters prosperity and security. Those boundaries have been critical to growing an incredible nation during our first two hundred years. As good as those boundaries have been for most of our nation's duration, they are now far too often neglected or completely overrun by overzealous politicians. Public gluttony has never worked, anytime, anywhere, and America is no different. We must get back to reality before our time in fantasyland ends or, as Margaret Thatcher put it, we run out of other people's money.

If Americans truly want to live in a republic that fosters independence from an abusive government, we must remind ourselves what the founding fathers wanted for America and fight to restore that vision through strict adherence and respect for the Constitution. This includes placing reasonable boundaries on government intrusions in our lives that deter our desire to live free and truly independent as our nation was intended to function. We must take a strong look at the proper role of government as the natural tendency of most in power is to expand their power until sufficient resistance is put in place to slow it down.

With reasonable boundaries in place where our elected officials respect the value of restraint, Americans will be able to focus more on what matters most: namely our faith, family, and community. Boundaries are valuable in all walks of life, and our Constitution provides an exceptional template intended for that purpose. A return to the principles in which these guidelines are followed instead of worked around will help America restore our path in a more successful direction. When we interact with our elected officials in communicating the value of boundaries, we must provide alternative solutions that provide more effective results. Examples may include:

- Families, not government, should be identified as the primary caretakers of our children;

- Businesses should be allowed to freely compete in the marketplace to provide valuable products and services without excessive or unfair taxation;

- Nonprofits, not government, should be the ones providing assistance for those in need as vested stakeholders in their causes; and

- Education should focus on teaching students the basics, including history and civics, without PC indoctrination.

As Dave Ramsay, founder of Financial Peace University and host of *The Dave Ramsey Show* says, debt is becoming one of our nation's greatest problems. Debt makes us vulnerable to others, and there are no shortcuts when it comes to getting out of it. This is true on a personal as well as a national level. If we are to put our financial house back in order, we must first take care of our debt, because nothing more pervasively undermines our prosperity, security, and economy than that. Living within our means provides us with peace, both at home and for our nation.

Establishing fairness in our tax policies is an effective way of reducing cronyism and favoritism. Any movement toward a flat tax would help eliminate much of the fiscal impropriety that damages our public sector. We can no longer afford to be shortsighted with our public policies and budgeting. In a nation that truly operates on a four-year cycle between elections, we have politicians eagerly offering us whatever they can to entice us to vote for them, and most of these promises provide some form of short-term value (at least perceived value), but these short-term gains come at a long-term cost. Have you ever noticed how much time is spent in Congress discussing bills while little is done to address the elephant in the room: how to reduce the insidious debt our nation has taken on? It will be interesting to observe the tax implications of the Trump administration's tax policies in the days ahead.

Other ideas for helping concerned citizens influence politicians to spend in a responsible manner include:

- Urge your elected officials to look long term in their policy decisions instead of for short-term political paybacks;

- Slow down the growth of government— as the current rate of taxation is simply unsustainable, as we know from Greece and other countries in world history;

- Request that your elected officials consider self-imposed term limits, which have the potential to help bring credibility and integrity to the political process without the concern of reelection factors; and

- Find responsible men and women who appreciate the opportunity to provide public-service leadership for intrinsic purposes instead of greed, power, and pay. (Then once they get elected, help keep them accountable to these principles.)

There is room in America for another Davy Crockett to arise and take on the challenge of public gluttony with a powerful, persuasive voice of reason and logic, combined with constraint to spend other people's money with wisdom instead of phony compassion. This person could be an elected official or even a civic leader. Wouldn't it be refreshing to have civic leaders call on our public officials to support their ever-expanding ideas with their own funds instead of continuous confiscation of our hard-earned money? With minimal hope in sight for slowing down public gluttony, we need a few honorable statesmen like Davy Crocket to come in and make persuasive arguments against our reckless spending of OPM before we officially go bankrupt as a nation.

> We know the way to prosperity. We just need the will to take it. We are in a mess, but we are comfortable in it as we rot on the inside of our nation in a manner which slowly eats away at our once-promising future and our infrastructure falls apart.
> —Kim Holmes, Heritage Foundation, from "Understanding American Prosperity," 11-29-12

- What do you think are some of the best ways you can effectively ask your elected officials to respect the taxpayers' limited resources and spend within their means?

- What steps do you think are necessary to have our government pay off its debts?

- Why do you think a flat/fair tax rate has not been adopted in America?

- What do you think are some of the primary reasons for the most prosperous nation in the world going $21-plus trillion in debt in such a short period of time?

- When do you think American taxation, currently at about 40 percent of GDP, will stop growing?

19. Regaining Our Lost Government

If ever time should come, when vain and aspiring men shall possess the highest seats in Government, our country will stand in need of its experienced patriots to prevent its ruin.
—*Samuel Adams*, political philosopher and founding father

America is in a battle for its cultural and political soul. To help give perspective on the magnitude of this challenge, I believe the best analogy we have for the fight facing our citizens is found in the biblical story of David versus Goliath. Yes, we the people face a very large beast in the explosion of government excess on so many levels. But just like in the David versus Goliath story, we the people can win this fight with persistence, courage, and, yes, a little help from God; OK, perhaps a lot of help from above. America is positioned to regain its lost government, but this fight will not be easy as politicians and their accomplices will fight to keep their power over us while citizens earnestly demand a government that serves us with respect.

The answer to regaining our lost government is not going to be found in electing more politicians from this party or that. The best answer lies in the hearts and minds of we the people to reconnect with the purpose and applicability of a constitutional republic in the twenty-first century. The answer is a focus on a new dialogue in which the divide between political power and civilian influence is reduced, and power returns to the vested stakeholders of our society. We need a changed narrative that it is OK to provide tough-love legislation, even if it means reducing the confiscation of some people's money to pay for the entitlements of others. We need to let church, family, and non-profits take care of people in need as they do it much better than the government, and the cost per result is much better. We need patriots who will be powerful voices for the principles that have established America as the greatest nation ever.

Abraham Lincoln stated in his famous Gettysburg Address in 1863 that Americans have a duty to ensure that "government of the people, by the people, for the people, shall not perish from the earth." Preserving the integrity of our nation is a noble cause, and change-oriented action is hard to create in large groups until the problem has been clearly identified and agreed to by enough leaders. Citizens often get frustrated about political movements that go against their views, but in the end, what really matters most is preserving a government that is truly of, by, and for the people. Our problem is that we have lost too many battles throughout our nation in the fight to maintain a civic-led government. A government by and for the people means empowering a stronger active citizen voice than what we have today in far too many power-hungry political arenas.

In our busy world, learning more about critical civic issues takes time, energy, and resources. In Erik Therwanger's incredible leadership book *The Leadership Connection*, he discusses how he helps people achieve powerful goals by encouraging them to focus on their core values and then tying their goals around them instead of just focusing on the overwhelming task at hand. In the same manner, civic engagement becomes a higher priority in our lives if we comprehend the immense value we provide for our families by doing our part to make our communities stronger. Being informed on the realities of the political world is one of the best returns on investment we can get. As government consumes nearly half our financial resources, it often operates with an ulterior motive that is detrimental to us, and the potential to have a positive impact is truly within our reach. The value of preserving a great nation affords us virtually unlimited opportunity to meet many personal goals.

The constitutional design of America is predicated on an actively engaged citizenry who carefully watch over their government. This intent is profound and powerful for an informed nation but can be challenging in today's culture. However, we need citizens with high moral character to stand up for the honorable American way of life before it gets taken away from all of us. Regaining our lost government requires civic leadership that incorporates these principles:

- Understanding that our government's problems are wide and deep and changing the status quo is a daunting challenge;

- Comprehending that transparency in public policy can be monitored in ways that best serve citizens, not by expanding the political system;

- Being able to speak boldly and with passion for the overall public good; and

- Being persuasive in incorporating the relevance of our Constitution and other time-tested virtues over personality conflicts that guide too many public officials in how they conduct their business.

Civic involvement has traditionally been defined as identifying how citizens can encourage their elected officials to support programs or policies that support their goals. It has traditionally focused on adding more power to the public sector. However, we now have a strong need for civic involvement that requires a different type of emphasis, one that focuses on the value of enhancing the private sector and charitable organizations while minimizing the growth and power of the public sector. The voices of accomplices asking for more political power significantly outweigh the restraints asked for by concerned citizens, and this needs to change for power to return to the citizens.

Most people believe repairing our federal government will not happen from inside the Beltway because there is strong resistance from the political elites and their accomplices to guard that power. Thus, perhaps the best way to overhaul Congress is from the outside. This approach was made possible by our founding fathers under Article 5 of our Constitution, which provides us with the option of calling for a Convention of States. Out of the twenty-seven amendments to our Constitution, this one has never been used, but there is significant movement toward this end, which can be found at www.ConventionofStates.com. In order to call together a Convention of States, two-thirds of the states (thirty-four) must call a convention proposing amendments. If thirty-four states call for it, Congress has no say on the convention, and all fifty states are represented in the process. This article is a safeguard for protecting America against an out-of-control government, and we are at a time when this process must be seriously considered as the best option for taking representation and power out of the hands of our political elites and putting it into the hands of we the people. The Convention of States movement provides three specific actions that could be powerful for bringing our country back to a true citizen-led government. These actions are:

- Impose fiscal restraints on the federal government;

- Limit its power and jurisdiction; and

- Impose term limits on its officials and members of Congress.

Congress has failed to manage our nation in a responsible manner, and the opportunity for citizens to regain control over our lost government may best be undertaken with this important option provided in our Constitution. Since Congress often creates laws from which it exempts itself and often fails to even establish a budget, perhaps this is the ideal time for citizens to demand that Congress follows the rules it sets for us via the calling of a Convention of States. I continue to marvel at how the principles covered in the articles of our Constitution provide hope and a path toward regaining a lost government during frustrating periods such as those we have before us today.

Beyond civic engagement directly with our elected officials, Americans can also change the course of our political direction through day-to-day discussions with our friends. I find too many political discussions end quickly and result in more frustration than agreement when they focus on which party is better for our nation or whether this politician is good or bad. Instead of continuing these frustrating arguments, perhaps we can engage in more productive discussions when we have the following conversations with those around us:

- Is the ideal American way one of individual independence or government dependence?

- What is productive rather than counterproductive to the American way?

- What is a good rather than a poor return on investment of limited taxpayer resources?

- What is lawful and moral rather than lawless and immoral?

- What provides long-term sustainability (e.g., infrastructure, defense, etc.) rather than short-term value (e.g., political appeasement)?

Politicians and their accomplices have gained power over the citizens of our country, and winning this rightful power back will not be easy. Though it will not be easy, we do have some incredible tools that can help us, if we can put them to good use. Critical citizen tools like our Constitution, Convention of States, open meeting laws, and elections can be used by an informed electorate to bring honorable public service principles back into practice where citizens regain control of our nation through a voice that is respected and accounted for through responsible government. America worked best for more than two hundred years when citizens ran this country, and the opportunity to regain control of our lost government is before us at this critical time in our nation's history.

> *The American dream comes from opportunity. The opportunity comes from our founding principles, our core values that's held together and protected by the Constitution. Those ideas are neither Republican, Democrat, conservative, liberal, white, or black. Those are American ideologies.*
>
> —Ted Yoho (R), US representative, Florida

★★★══ QUESTIONS TO PONDER

- What do you think are some of the most reasonable options for citizens to regain our lost government from the political elites and their accomplices?

- What are the key trigger points that necessitate urgency in making this happen before it's too late?

- How can technology help bring real-time public accountability closer to our citizens?

- What values motivate you the most to become more active in civics?

20. Bringing Hope to the Next Generation

Patriotic—to encourage an understanding of American heritage, civic responsibilities, love of country, and willingness to defend it.

—One of five stated goals of the College of the
Ozarks, Missouri

The future of America belongs to our younger generation. America's millennials have been defined in many ways, good and bad. What I see in the next generation is an excitement to improve the world around them but little background in the great heritage of this country. In their defense, our younger generation has not been as intimately involved in observing the sacrifices made by the earlier generations who protected us in two world wars or even the relatively recent terrorist attacks on our nation in 2001. But there is hope, and I believe the older generation owes it to the younger to hand down some of the principles that have helped shape this nation in some exceptional ways. These impressionable millennials eagerly want mentors to show them what form of government serves a higher value, our constitutional form of government or the socialist styles of government they are frequently taught in many of our schools today. It is up to us to show them the incredible values and unlimited opportunities brought forth by America's unique, time-tested virtues of limited government.

As I spoke across the nation in support of my first book, *Fixing America's Shattered Politics*, I was blessed to see the heartbeat of America thrive in many special places. The true heartbeat of America is Main Street USA, which provides unlimited opportunity for future generations to pursue their dreams. But this exceptional place will only be available for our children and grandchildren to enjoy if we do our part now to preserve freedom and liberty throughout America.

One place I found during my travels that embodies the values of our American heritage while teaching young adults incredible life-changing skills they can use in the marketplace is College of the Ozarks in Branson, Missouri. This amazing place has earned the nickname "Hard Work U." Students attend college free of charge while committing to working on campus fifteen hours per week. When I visited its beautiful campus, I was greeted by some of the most respectful, helpful student-workers, who took great pride in their school and their jobs. It was obvious this school placed a strong emphasis on respectfully serving people who visit. Branson offers many other reasons to visit as well, and it means a lot that one of the highest-rated activities in the area on TripAdvisor is College of the Ozarks. Their restaurant, staffed by students, is ranked the best in town, and the hotel is ranked the fourth-best on-campus hotel in the United States. This is truly an incredible place that emphasizes patriotism and many other valuable real-life lessons for our youth.

Setting the vision at this campus is President Jerry C. Davis, who is committed to establishing and preserving high standards for these students. His philosophy is that it is difficult to gain entrance into Hard Work U, but it is easy to get kicked out for those who do not meet the standards expected of them. Isn't this the reality of how all of life works? Bringing a promising future forward with our next generation will need to be fully immersed in reality, where discipline and dedication to overcoming real-life obstacles make us stronger. Isn't this what education and life are all about?

Another example that provides inspiration for our youth is the American Legion's Boys and Girls State programs. These week-long summer courses in Americanism and civics provide an incredible opportunity for high school seniors to learn more about how they can be effective civic leaders and/or elected officials. This program is provided in every state across the United States except Hawaii and is attended by thousands each summer. I was blessed with the opportunity to speak at one of these programs, and the passion exhibited by the staff and students involved inspires great hope for these future leaders of our great nation. Our nation's future is stronger when public service principles based on honor and integrity are taught to our next generation.

One of the more inspiring charitable organizations that fills an important void for our honorable service members is the Eagle's Healing Nest, a home for homeless disabled veterans. This incredible organization provides a place of healing and recovery for our military as they return home from our nations' battles in need of help on their journey back to civilian life. Like all incredible organizations, it has a strong leader in Melony Butler who built this refuge for our military heroes with a powerful vision of "Promises made…promises kept," which guides her in her care for these veterans. She wants to do her part to make sure our military heroes are provided a place of transition in a safe environment, and the facility now houses more than a hundred veterans in two Minnesota locations with no paid staff. The

Eagle's Healing Nest is an incredible testament to how effective a non-profit can be in passionately addressing a large gap in the social needs of our nation. Going back to Davy Crockett's persuasive speech before Congress, the Eagle's Healing Nest is a modern-day example of charity taking on an extremely challenging situation and providing unbelievable results with minimal government assistance.

Another great organization that utilizes many patriotic volunteers to serve our military is the United Service Organization (USO). The Seattle/Tacoma area USO in particular has incredible patriots who go beyond the call of duty to serve our service members with passion and purpose. This USO includes a radio program that promotes local support of various veteran needs, which are then supported by their listeners. I was blessed with the opportunity to speak on their USO radio program and meet with many of these outstanding service members. This initiative was supported by Honor Flight Twin Cities, which expanded its mission to include bringing patriotic lessons learned by our older generation to our younger genera-tion, in addition to bringing World War II veterans to their monument in DC twice each year.

Love and hope are two virtues that are deeply admired by humanity. We desire to be loved, and it is a blessing to love others. Beyond love, humans are always looking for hope to overcome challenging situations. As I lis-ten to the heartbeat of America, I hear tremendous angst about the divi-sions going on across America, and many are losing hope that we can turn around this deep mess we are in. The challenge of restoring a divided America is daunting, and overcoming this tremendous breakdown seems overwhelming in many ways. But we can, and frankly, we must take on this beast of burden for preserving the future of our great nation.

America truly is the great place of opportunity for all. The blessings of freedom, liberty, and justice that we have enjoyed have been handed over to us by our predecessors through much perspiration and sacrifice, and it is now our responsibility to pass these blessings on to future generations. Adversity is a great teacher for those who want to learn from it and overcome the next challenge. For me, my political experience was in many ways not very enjoyable as I saw the ugly side of politics, which contrasted so intensely with the more honorable public service attributes I had previously learned in the military. The key for all of us is learning from these challenges and being able to stay focused on the efforts needed to achieve victory during dark days. We have a major mess on our hands in our shattered political world, where few can find hope for turning things around. If we can learn from the mistakes made in today's shattered political arena, we will take a huge step in the right direction.

Hope begins with clear sight of our dreams and a realistic path toward fulfilling those dreams. I believe the best place for making our dreams come true is right here in the United States of America. After all, aren't we here to pursue a meaningful life for ourselves and our loved ones? You see, people will do most anything for someone they love when they can make a positive difference. There is hope for America's future if enough concerned citizens come together with trust in the principles that formed our nation and fortitude to stay focused on bringing common sense and decency back into our culture where we move forward as one nation, under God, indivisible, with liberty and justice for all. Leaving the legacy of a stronger nation would be a great gift for our children and grandchildren, wouldn't it?

> *Now more than ever before, the people are responsible for the character of their Congress. If that body be ignorant, reckless and corrupt, it is because the people tolerate ignorance, recklessness and corruption. If it be intelligent, brave and pure, it is because the people demand these high qualities to represent them in the national legislature…If the next centennial does not find us a great nation…it will be because those who*

represent the enterprise, the culture, and the morality of the nation do not aid in controlling the political forces.

—James Garfield, twentieth president of the United

States, 1877

★★★▬▬▬ QUESTIONS TO PONDER

- What do you think is most important for restoring hope with our youngest generations?

- Which organizations do you believe can have the most impact on bringing honor and integrity back into the public sector?

- How do you see yourself making an impact in shaping the future of your community?

V

Conclusion

Hold on, my friends, to the Constitution and to the Republic for which it stands. Miracles do not cluster, and what has happened once in 6,000 years, may not happen again. Hold on to the Constitution, for if the American Constitution should fail, there will be anarchy throughout the world.

—Daniel Webster, former US representative and senator who represented New Hampshire from 1813 to 1817 and Massachusetts from 1823 to 1841

America shines brightly as a beacon of light for the rest of the world to see how a virtuous principle of "one nation, under God, with liberty and justice for all" can inspire humanity to greatness. The true test of greatness for any individual or organization is having moral character in place to overcome adversity. America has withstood tremendous adversity many times throughout its incredible history with strong leadership by brave men and women with great virtues. However, the crumbling of a nation is always just one generation away, and we are dangerously close to losing the sustainability and vitality of a nation that has provided so many Americans with blessings that we too often take for granted. But our children, our grandchildren, and our great-grandchildren need us now to proactively right the sinking ship of America through civic leadership, personal courage, and moral persuasion in a manner that brings America back to the foundational values that have proven to be worthy of great sacrifice.

In many ways, the return of America to a place where individual independence is greater than government dependence is a daunting challenge that will be very difficult to attain. However, Americans love a great fight, and with focus on the prize that awaits us with victory for freedom and liberty, we can restore hope for America's future.

As we learn in the military, freedom is not free, and service never ends. The more rights we give away to an abusive government, the less freedom and the fewer choices we have as individuals. The bottom line is that the price of freedom is eternal vigilance by a nation devoted and loyal to protecting our national treasure, the United States of America, and all the greatness that it stands for throughout our darkened world. Although I am now retired from military service, I continue to be inspired as I observe the incredible sacrifices made by so many brave men and women in uniform who defend this nation. Our military does an exceptional job of defending our nation with honor and integrity in many powerful ways. While our military is protecting us in many mighty ways, far too many of our politicians are not. If we can just bring some of these honorable military virtues into our political arena, I believe hardworking citizens would regain some level of desperately needed trust in our elected officials. Let's do our part to make politicians earn our trust by incorporating our newly-expanded Crawl, Walk, Run civic principles going forward, including:

- Crawl – by solidifying how our personal core values relate to the incredible privileges associated with being an American citizen;

- Walk – into a public forum and observe public business taking place and speak up, if necessary, to ensure business is conducted in a professional, respectful manner which focuses on the overall public good; and

- Run – by effectively utilizing your new civic leadership tools to make a positive impact throughout your sphere of influence.

You are a vital stakeholder in the future of this great country. America needs your civic leadership to become an even greater nation. Congratulations on completing this book. As you go forward with purpose within your sphere of influence in guiding our nation using your God-given talents, passions, and abilities, remember that there are plenty of opportunities available to make a positive impact in restoring hope across America, including:

- Embracing your family with love and encouragement to accept personal responsibility and become productive members of your community;

- Providing support for charities and churches that are doing great things to help those in need;

- Supporting patriotic citizens who speak out for decency throughout America;

- Mentoring our younger generation by helping them grow with great principles that guide their way toward healthy self-actualization;

- Thanking civic watchdogs who actively observe our government at work and bring indiscretions to our attention; and

- Supporting elected officials who desire to serve with honor and integrity to make the best decisions possible in a manner that is most fair for all involved, including both givers and takers of our limited resources.

May God bless you as you go forward with serving God, protecting your family, and preserving the American way of life for this and future generations to enjoy as the land of the free, home of the brave! As you continue in your journey as a civic leader, following are several patriotic reminders of the great heritage we have as Americans, including:

- America's National Anthem;
- The American's Creed;
- America's Pledge of Allegiance; and
- Example Test Questions on American Citizenship, as administered by US Citizenship & Immigration Services.

America's National Anthem

(First stanza from The Star-Spangled Banner)

Oh, say, can you see, by the dawn's early light
What so proudly we hail'd at the twilight's last gleaming?
Whose broad stripes and bright stars, through the perilous fight
O'er the ramparts we watch'd, were so gallantly streaming?
And the rockets' red glare, the bombs bursting in air
Gave proof through the night that our flag was still there
O say, does that star-spangled banner yet wave
O'er the land of the free and the home of the brave!

—Francis Scott Key

The American's Creed

"I believe in the United States of America as a Government of the people by the people, for the people, whose just powers are derived from the consent of the governed; a democracy in a Republic; a sovereign Nation of many sovereign States; a perfect Union, one and inseparable; established upon those principles of freedom, equality, justice, and humanity for which American patriots sacrificed their lives and fortunes.

I therefore believe it is my duty to my Country to love it; to support its Constitution; to obey its laws; to respect its flag, and to defend it against all enemies."

—William Tyler Page, 1917 (adopted by US House of Representatives as *"The American's Creed"* on April 13, 1918.

America's Pledge of Allegiance

"I pledge allegiance to the Flag of the United States of America, and to the Republic for which it stands, one Nation under God, indivisible, with liberty and justice for all."

—As formally adopted by Congress in 1945; the most recent addition, "under God," was added in 1954

US Citizenship and Immigration Services (USCIS) Testing[27]

Becoming a stronger American means knowing what our nation is truly all about. The following is a sampling of questions that those wishing to become American citizens take as part of their application to become legal US citizens. This test includes a random sample of 50 of the 100 questions used by the USCIS for applicants who filed for naturalization on or after October 1, 2008. In order to become eligible for US citizenship, applicants must have answered at least 60 percent correctly.

1. What is the supreme law of the land?

2. What does the Constitution do?

3. The idea of self-government is in the first three words of the Constitution. What are these words?

4. What is an amendment?

5. What do we call the first ten amendments of the Constitution?

6. What is one right or freedom from the First Amendment?

7. How many amendments does the Constitution have?

8. What did the Declaration of Independence do?

9. What are two rights in the Declaration of Independence?

10. What is freedom of religion?

11. What is the economic system of the United States?

12. What is the "rule of law"?

13. Name one branch of the government.

14. What stops one branch of government from becoming too powerful?

15. Who is in charge of the executive branch?

16. Who makes federal laws?

17. What are the two parts of Congress?

18. How many US senators are there?

19. Who is one of your state's US senators?

20. Name your US representative.

21. Why do some states have more representatives than other states?

22. We elect a president for how many years?

23. In what month do we vote for president?

24. If the president can no longer serve, who becomes president?

25. Who is the commander in chief of the military?

26. What does the president's cabinet do?

27. What does the judicial branch do?

28. What is the highest court in the US?

29. Who is the governor of your state?

30. What is the capital of your state?

31. What is one responsibility that is only for US citizens?

32. What are two rights of everyone living in the US?

33. What do we show loyalty to when we say the Pledge of Allegiance?

34. What is one promise you make when you become a US citizen?

35. How old do citizens have to be to vote for president?

36. What are two ways Americans can participate in their democracy?

37. When is the last day you can send in federal income tax forms?

38. What is one reason colonists came to America?

39. Who wrote the Declaration of Independence?

40. When was the Declaration of Independence adopted?

41. When was the Constitution written?

42. Who was the first president?

43. Name the US war between the North and the South.

44. Name one problem that led to the Civil War.

45. What did Susan B. Anthony do?

46. Name one war fought by the US in the 1900s.

47. What major event happened on September 11, 2001, in the US?

48. What is the capital of the US?

49. What is the name of the national anthem?

50. Name two national US holidays.

NOTES

1. US Citizenship and Immigration Services, *"Naturalization Oath of Allegiance to the United States of America,"* *https://www.uscis.gov/us-citizenship/naturalization-test/ naturalization-oath-allegiance-united-states-america.*

2. Angela Dewan, Vasco Cotavio and Hillary Clarke, CNN, *"Catalonia independence referendum: What just happened?"* *https://www.cnn. com/2017/10/02/europe/catalonia-independence-referendum-explainer/ index.html,* October 2, 2017.

3. Thomas Jefferson, *"First Inaugural Address,"* Teaching American History.org: *http://teachingamericanhistory.org/library/document/first-in-augural-address-8/,* March 4, 1801.

4. Kim Holmes, *Understanding American Prosperity* (Heritage Foundation: *https://www.heritage.org/international-economies/report/ understanding-american-prosperity,* 11-29-12).

5. David Azerrad, *"Five Great Virtues that Make Americans Amazing,"* The Daily Signal: *https://www.dailysignal.com/2011/07/03/five-great-virtues-that-make-americans-amazing/,* July 3, 2011.

6. Andrea Diaz, CNN, *"Take a knee protests go from the sidelines to City Council chambers,"* *https://www.cnn.com/2017/10/18/us/city-leaders-take-a-knee-during-pledge-of-allegiance-trnd/index.html,* October 18, 2017.

7. Mila Koumpilova, *"Hennepin County sets out to fund legal help for immigrants,"* Star Tribune: *http://www.startribune.com/hennepin-county-sets-out-to-fund-legal-help-for-immigrants/477877153/*, March 25, 2018).

8. Isanti-Chisago County Star, *"New commish off to rocky start, http://www.isanti-chisagocountystar.com/new-commish-off-to-rocky-start/article_8dae35d3-c695-56b5-b923-da8bce1ff482.html*, February 17, 2009.

9. Isanti-Chisago County Star, *"Commissioner Duff responds to Mr. Sheppard," http://www.isanti-chisagocountystar.com/commissioner-duff-re-sponds-to-mr-sheppard/article_5c19811f-e946-5ac2-bc4b-6997615e02d7.html*, March 4, 2009.

10. Kim Holmes, *Understanding American Prosperity* (Heritage Foundation: *https://www.heritage.org/international-economies/report/understanding-american-prosperity*, 11-29-12).

11. Milton Friedman, *"Milton Friedman vs Free Lunch Advocate,"* Common Sense Capitalism: https://www.youtube.com/watch?v=9Qe7fL-L25AQ, March 4, 2014.

12. Star Parker, *"America's Generosity is Unmatched,"* Real Clear Politics: https://www.realclearpolitics.com/articles/2008/06/americas_generos-ity_is_unmatch.html, June 3, 2008.

13. *Dr. Eric Ostermeier, "America Held Hostage: The Political Rhetoric of Barack Obama,"* (Smart Politics: http://editions.lib.umn.edu/smartpoli-tics/2013/02/08/america-held-hostage-the-polit/, February 8, 2013.

14. Joseph Curl, *"Poll: 85% of Americans Think Free Speech More Important Than Political Correctness,"* (The Daily Wire, *https://www.daily-wire.com/news/20162/poll-85-americans-think-free-speech-more-import-ant-joseph-curl*, August 24, 2017).